Training for Rowing

Ed McNeely M.Sc.
Sport Performance Institute
Ottawa, Ontario
Canada

ISBN: 0-9682104-1-4

Sport Performance Institute Inc.
1769 St. Laurent Blvd. Suite 133
Ottawa, CN
K1G 5X7

1. 888. 780. 7741
613. 825. 6909

Contents

1 Warm Up — **11**

2 Aerobic Training Categories — **23**

3 Determining Aerobic Training Categories — **57**

4 Introduction to Planning and Periodization — **85**

5 Periodized Model of Strength Training for Rowers — **105**

Contents

6   Strength Training for Prepubescent Rowers   **125**

7   Teaching Weight Training and Skill Development   **139**

8   Flexibility Training   **157**

9   Tapering   **173**

10   Nutritional Ergogenics and Rowing   **183**

Contents

11	Weight Loss and Making Weight	211
12	Nutritional Requirements of Rowing	223
	Index	256

Dedication

To mom and dad
for all the years of support and encouragement

Acknowledgements

I would like to thank the coaches that have listened to me over the years and who have taught me about the sport of rowing. Al Morrow, Volker Nolte, Brian Richardson, and Jim Joy have been especially helpful with their views and ideas on rowing.
I also need to thank the Canadian National Team athletes who over the years have asked very thought provoking questions and forced me to be thorough and keep on top current training practices and techniques.

Preface

Over the past eight years I have worked as a consultant to the Canadian National Rowing Team. During this time I have had the priveledge of meeting and learning from some of the best rowing coaches in the world. I haver also had the opportunity to work with rowers and clubs from across Canada and the United States.

This book provides many of the answers to the common questions that I hear when consulting with both coaches and athletes. This book is the culmination of many years work and I think it can best be summed up in the following statement:

"Ed McNeely has produced a book which is scientifically sound, based on the history and best practices of the Canadian National Rowing Team, yet which is accesssible to any rower in the most remote reaches of Canada. The book is transparent, a deceptive simplicity, clear to those who are not exercise physiologists, and with methods of testing which are accessible to all. All rowing nations and all levels of rowing will benefit from this discussion of rowing physiology and testing. I am particularly interested in this becoming the Bible of club rowing in Canada."

Dr. Richard Backus
Chairman
Rowing Canada Sport Science
and Medicine Committee

I hope it helps improve both you performance and enjoyment of rowing

Ed McNeely, M.Sc.
President
Sport Performance Institute Inc.

10

Warm Up

1

Warming up prior to exercising or competing is widely recommended. It is suggested that warming up can improve performance and prevent injury. The necessity of warming up, however, remains in question (Fox, Bowers and Foss, 1989).

The Necessity of Warming Up

Is a warm up necessary prior to training? Some studies show no difference in performing with or without a warm up (Karpovich and Hale, 1956; Mathews and Snyder, 1959; Skubic and Hodgkins, 1957) while others have found warming up beneficial to performing (Ingjer and Stromme, 1979; Berg and Ekblom, 1979; Michael, Skubic and Rochelle, 1957; Pacheco, 1957). Factors other than a warm up's physical effects could account for the discrepancies in performance benefits seen in the literature. Psychological factors, experience of the subjects, and the type of warm up can all affect the results of studies. To determine the necessity of warming up, the resulting physiological benefits should be examined.

The Physiological Effects of Warming up

Increased Temperature

An increase in body temperature is one of the main physiological adaptations to warming up. The increase results from non-utilized energy and dissipated heat produced by friction from sliding muscle filaments during contraction (Elam, 1986). The elevated temperature results in a more rapid and complete dissociation of oxygen from hemoglobin (Barcroft and King 1909) enhancing oxidative processes in the muscle (Shellock, 1983) and increasing VO2 max. Increased body temperature stimulates vasodilation in the working muscle increasing blood flow through the muscle (Shellock, 1983) and reduced muscle viscosity increasing mechanical efficiency (Shellock, 1983). Nerve conduction velocity is improved (Martin et al., 1975) resulting in faster contractions and relaxation of muscles (Tipton and Karpovich, 1966; Fisher and Jensen, 1990). The heart rate increases and lactic acid production decreases after warming up (Martin et al. 1979; Ingjer and Stromme, 1979).

Cardiac Adaptations

Heart problems such as myocardial ischemia, arrythmias, and sudden cardiac death can occur during exercise (Siscovick, 1990). These problems tend to occur most often in middle-aged and older men (Vouri, 1984). When exercise is combined with other coronary risk factors such as hypertension, cigarette smoking, obesity, and high cholesterol the risk of exercise related cardiac problems increases (Siscovick, 1990).

Warming up, however, may help prevent serious damage to the heart (Elam,1986). Barnard et al. (1973) reported that 68% of their subjects, men aged 21 to 52, experienced abnormal ECG readings when they exercised without warming up. Jogging easily for two minutes before the training session though eliminated the abnormal ECG readings in most subjects and reduced it in the others. Abnormal readings seen during training without a warm up have been attributed to the inability of coronary blood flow to meet the demands that the exercise session places on the heart muscle (Barnard et al.,1973b).

Injury Prevention

Preventing injuries, such as muscle strains and tears, is often suggested as one of the primary benefits of warming up (Elam,1986; Shellock,1983; Bompa,1983). Even though these authors suggest warming up can help prevent injuries, they are quick to point out that most of the evidence is empirical and very few, if any, studies show that warming up decreases the incidence of musculoskeletal injuries. This is in part because during a study a researcher would never set out to injure his or her subjects intentionally. It is hypothesized that warming up can help prevent injuries because it stretches the muscle tendon unit resulting in a greater length for a given load; this places less tension on the muscle-tendon junction reducing the potential for injury (Stone, 1992).

Types of Warm Ups

There are three types of warm ups: passive, general and specific. Each has its advantages and disadvantages.

Passive Warm Up

A passive warm up increases temperature through external means. Massage, hot showers, lotions, and heating pads are common forms (Bompa, 1983; Shellock, 1983). Although these methods increase body temperature, they produce little positive effect on performance. Ingjer and Stromme (1979) compared the effects of active, passive and no warm up on physiological markers of performance. They found that the passive warm up did not increase VO2, or decrease blood lactate levels any more than no warm up. They did find, however, that the heart rate increased. Stanley et al. (1994) found no increase in strength performance following hot water baths. A passive warm up, because of increased muscle temperature, may be suitable prior to a stretching exercise but should not be recommended as the sole means of warming up for intense physical activity.

General Warm Up

A general warm up increases temperature by using movements for the major muscle groups. Calisthenics and light jogging activities are most common (Bompa, 1983; Shellock, 1983). This type of warm up is meant to increase temperature in a variety of muscles using general movement patterns. Such a warm up is good for a fitness class, but should not serve as the sole form of warm up for athletic training of events.

Specific Warm Up

The specific warm up is designed to prepare the participant for the specific demands of the upcoming activity. The specific warm up helps psychological readiness, co-ordination of specific movement patterns, and prepares the central nervous system (Bompa, 1983). A specific warm up usually consists of a simulation of some technical component of the activity at work rates that increase progressively. For example, an Olympic weightlifter will perform the snatch with heavier weights progressively until reaching 80-90% of the opening attempt. Shellock (1983) suggested that because of the rehearsal component of this type of warm up, it is the preferred method.

Designing a Warm Up

Stretching

There is some controversy over what a warm up should consist of and when it should be performed. Although it is generally agreed that stretching should be included in a warm up, there is disagreement as to when it should be included. Most fitness classes have a warm up consisting of general full body aerobic movements followed by a stretching component. Several researchers and strength coaches recommend this progression (Bompa, 1983; Shellock, 1983; Allerheiligen and Rogers, 1995) based on the fact that temperature affects the flexibility of tendons and ligaments. Vigorously stretching a cold muscle may result in injury; however, this is unproven (Jones, Rock, and Moore, 1988).

Stretching is also recommended as the first part of a warm up prior to exercising or testing (Fox, Bowers and Foss, 1989; Gettman, 1988). This progression is used by competitive weightlifters and powerlifters as well as other athletic groups (Robbins, 1993; Duvall, 1993). Again there is no evidence that light stretching before aerobic activity will result in muscle or tendon injury.

Duration of warm up

The amount of time needed to warm up depends on the type and intensity of the activity as well as environmental conditions. For someone engaged in a light jogging program 10 minutes may be sufficient for a warm up. Elite level athletes may require 30 or 40 minutes to warm up depending on the nature of the event (Shellock, 1983; Bompa, 1983). Exercising in a warm environment requires a shorter warm up than exercising in a cold one. In a normal environment the onset of sweating is usually a good indicator that body temperature has increased sufficiently (Shellock, 1983).

Warming up for strength and power events

As mentioned, athletes in strength and power events seem to prefer to begin their warm up with light stretching. Whether this is the most efficient way to warm up is still a topic for debate. The final part of a warm up for these events should be a specific warm up (Shellock, 1983; Bompa, 1983).

When weight training, do at least two sets, one at 50% and one at 75% of the work weight, before using the working weight. Very strong people need to do more sets. This author has seen elite powerlifters use six to eight warm up sets prior to opening attempts in competition.

Pre-race Warm up for Rowing

A well-designed warm up has the following components:

1. Stretching
2. Light row
3. Hard strokes
4. Light row

Stretching

Often warm up stretches are confused with stretching to increase flexibility. Stretching during a warm up is designed to help an athlete reach an existing level of flexibility. This stretching also activates the stretch receptors in the joints and muscles. This may help the athlete row technically better. Warm up stretches should be held for 10 seconds. Stretches should be both general and rowing specific. This portion of the warm up should take 10 to 15 minutes.

Light Row

This the first of two light rows is designed to increase body temperature and provide the performance benefits listed above. This is a good time to mentally rehearse the race and think about the strategy. This portion of the warm up should last 15 to 20 minutes. If it isn't possible to be on the water this long prior to the race an ergometer or running can be used to raise temperature instead.

Hard Strokes

Doing hard strokes or short sprints helps increase muscle temperature, improves lactic acid removal, and gives the crew the feeling of speed and power going into the start. The sprint period or hard strokes should not be done for more than 15 seconds at a time. Longer periods may result in lactic acid accumulation that could slow race performance. The total time spent doing hard strokes should be about five minutes.

Light Row

Following the hard strokes five to 10 minutes of light paddling will help remove any lactic acid that has built up and prevent fatigue from setting in early in the race. This is the part of the warm up that is most often forgotten, but may be the most important for race performance.

A good warm up prior to a race will take 35 to 60 minutes. Individual differences exist between athletes as to how long they need. Environmental conditions such as temperature and humidity also play a role in warm up duration. On a cool fall or spring day, warm up may have to be substantially longer than on a hot humid summer day. Combine the recommendations made here with your own judgement to make sure you get the most out of your pre-race preparation.

Conclusion

Warm ups, when designed properly, can improve performance in both aerobic and anaerobic events. The type, intensity and duration of a warm up depends on the nature of the activity and environmental conditions. Although there is still some argument about the order of activities in a warm up there should be a stretching, temperature raising and specific component.

References

Allerheiligen, B., and Rogers, R. (1995). Plyometrics program design. Strength and Conditioning. 17(4): 26-31.

Barcroft, J., and King, W., (1909). The effect of temperature on the dissociation curve of blood. Journal of Physiology London. 39: 374-384.

Barnard, R., et al. (1973). Cardiovascular responses to sudden strenuous exercise: heart rate, blood pressure, and ECG .
Journal of Applied Physiology. 34: 833-837.
Barnard, R., et al. (1973b). Ischemic response to sudden strenuous exercise in healthy men. Circulation. 48: 936-942.

Berg, U., and Ekblom, B. (1979). Physical performance and peak aerobic power at different body temperatures. Journal of Applied Physiology. 46(5): 885-889.

Bompa, T. (1983). Theory and Methodology of Training: The key to Athletic Performance. Dubuque, Iowa: Kendall/Hunt Publishing Company.

Duvall, M. (1993). Implementing plyometrics in an in -season football program. NSCA Journal.15(3): 57-59.

Elam, R. (1986). Warm-up and athletic performance: a physiological analysis. NSCA Journal. 8(2):30

Fisher, A., and Jensen, C. (1990). Scientific Basis of Athletic Conditioning. Lea & Febiger. Philadelphia, PA.

Fox, E., Bowers, R., and Foss, M. (1989). The Physiological Basis of Physical Education and Athletics.Wm C. Brown Publishers. Dubuque, Iowa.

Gettman, L. (1988). Fitness Testing. In Resource Manual for Guidelines for Exercise Testing and Prescription. Lea & Febiger. Philadelphia, PA.

Ingjer, F , and Stromme, S.B. (1979). Effects of active, passive or no warm up on the physiological response to heavy exercise. European Journal of Applied Physiology. 40: 273-282.

Jones, B., Rock, P., and Moore, M. (1988). Musculoskeletal injury: risks prevention , and first aid. In Resource Manual for Guidelines for Exercise Testing and Prescription. Lea & Febiger. Philadelphia, PA.

Karpovich, P and Hale, C. (1956). Effect of warm up on physical performance. Journal of the American Medical Association. 162: 1117-1119.

Martin, B., Robinson, S., Wiegman, D., and Aulick, L. (1979). Effects of warm up on metabolic responses to strenuous exercise.Medicine and Science in Sports. 7(2): 146-149.

Mathews, D and Snyder, H. (1959). Effects of warm up on the 440 yard dash. Research Quarterly. 30: 446-451.

Michael, E., Skubic, V., and Rochelle, R., (1957). Effect of warm up on softball throw for distance. Research Quarterly. 30: 446-451.

Pacheco, B., (1957). Improvement in jumping performance due to preliminary exercise. Research Quarterly. 28: 55-63.

Robbins, P. (1993). A pre-season strength training program for high school wrestlers. National Strength and Conditioning Association Journal. 15(3): 62-64.

Shellock, F. (1983). Physiological benefits of warm up. The Physician and Sports Medicine. 11(10): 134-139.

Siscovick, D. (1990). Risks of exercising: Sudden cardiac death and injuries. In Exercise, Fitness, and Health A Consensus of Current Knowledge. Bouchard, Shephard, Stephens, Sutton, and McPherson Editors. Human Kinetics Books. Champaign, Ill. 707-714.

Aerobic Training Categories

2

24

Competitive race rowing lasts for five to 12 minutes over a 2000 m course. During this time 70 to 80% of the energy used is produced by aerobic metabolism. This sort of demand makes aerobic training the most crucial aspect of the physical preparation rowers.

The American College of Sports Medicine recommends 15 to 60 minutes of exercise at 40 to 85% of VO_2 max three to five days per week for improving health and cardiorespiratory fitness (ACSM, 1991). While this type of a recommendation is acceptable for people who wish to lead an active lifestyle and improve their health it may not be beneficial for those with specific fitness or performance goals.

The range of potential exercise intensities that may be considered aerobic varies from a casual stroll down the street to an all out performance in a 1500 m running race. Because of this range, and the fact that aerobic training adaptations adhere to the concept of specificity of training, sport scientists and coaches have designed training category systems to facilitate the development of more accurate and specific aerobic training programs. Training categories are used by most top-level endurance athletes worldwide. While the naming schemes used may vary from country to country, or even from sport to sport, the physiological basis for the training categories is the same.

Physiological Basis of Training Categories

A training category system is based on three physiological points; aerobic threshold, anaerobic threshold, and VO_2 max. Figure 1 shows the relationship of these points to each other. Before the training categories can be used effectively it is necessary to understand where they come from.

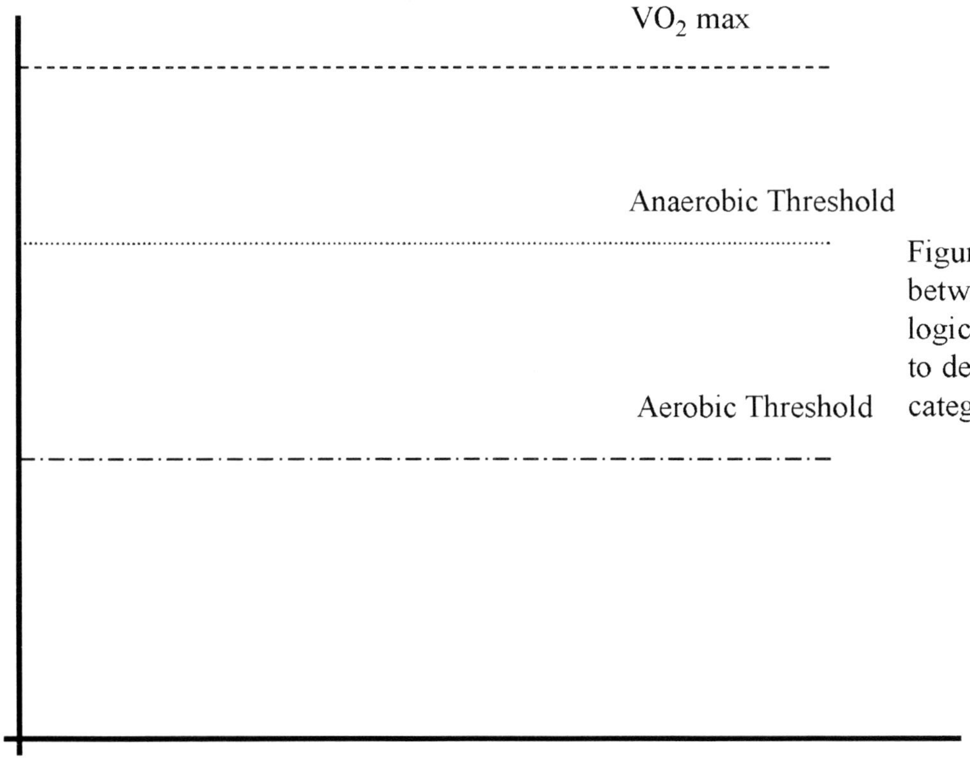

Figure 1. Relationship between three physiological variables used to determine training categories

Training categories are based on the levels of blood lactic acid that accumulate during exercise. Lactic acid is a product of anaerobic glycolysis. If allowed to accumulate within the tissue lactic acid can contribute rapidly to fatigue. It does this by decreasing blood pH and interfering with energy production, altering membrane permeability or interfering with calcium ion binding at the actomyosin binding sites (Wenger and Reed, 1976).

If exercise intensity is gradually increased from very light loads up to maximal loads, blood levels of lactic acid follow a pattern similar to that in figure 2. It is from a chart like this that aerobic threshold and anaerobic threshold are determined.

The Concept of Thresholds

The concepts of aerobic and anaerobic threshold are continually being debated in the scientific literature. Many investigators believe there really is no threshold point (Yeh et al. 1983; Hughson et al. 1987; Brooks, 1985), while others clearly believe there are distinctive threshold points (Davis, 1985; Antonutto and Diprampero, 1995; Stegman, Kindermann, and Schnabel, 1981). Part of the debate is simply a matter of semantics. Researchers have questioned the validity of the term 'anaerobic' while others have questioned the term 'threshold.' Part of the reason for the debate is that a number of different ways have been proposed for the determination of aerobic and anaerobic threshold (Orr, Green, Hughson, and Bennett, 1982; Beaver, Wasserman, and Whip, 1986; Heck et al. 1985; Kinndermann and Schnabel, 1981). It has been suggested that the technology is not yet available to precisely pinpoint a single intensity that can be termed aerobic or anaerobic threshold.

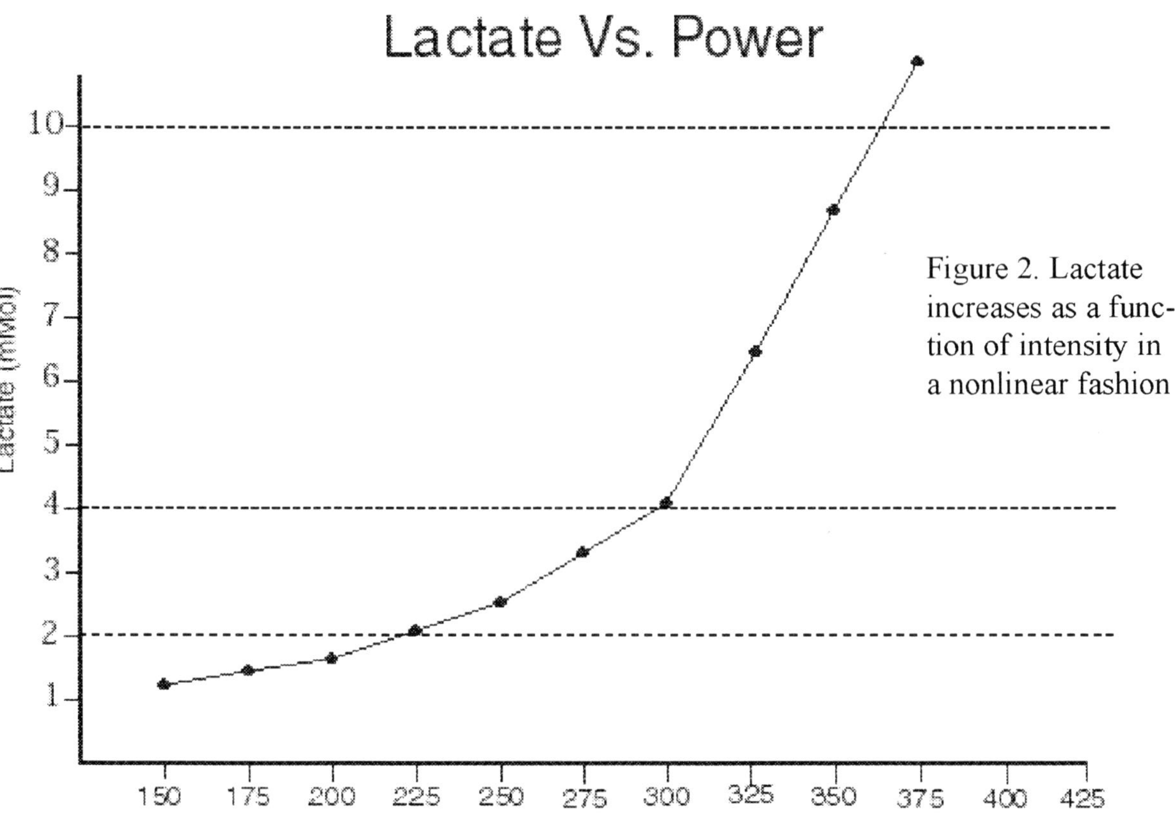

Figure 2. Lactate increases as a function of intensity in a nonlinear fashion

While scientists continue to argue the fine points of threshold determination there is little debate as to the value of the concepts embodied by these threshold points (Thoden, 1991). The development of training categories resolves much of the debate about the threshold points by prescribing a range of intensities for exercise. For those with further interest on the threshold debate please see the articles by Brooks (1985) and Davis (1985).

Aerobic Threshold

The aerobic threshold has been defined as the point just below the level of energy metabolism where blood lactate concentration increases distinctly from its resting level (Aunola and Rusko, 1986). It is also the exercise level below which the great majority of the muscle fibres are working aerobicly (Antonutto and DiPrampero, 1995). This point is generally seen to occur around 2mMol of lactate (Antonutto and DiPrampero, 1995; Kindermann , Simon, and Keul, 1979; Skinner and McLellan, 1980).

The aerobic threshold occurs because of a change in the type of muscle fibre recruited during the activity. During lower intensity exercise the slow twitch muscle fibres are recruited (Henneman, 1957; Burke, 1986). As the intensity of exercise increases more muscle fibres are activated. When slow twitch fibres can no longer handle the required workload fast twitch fibres are activated. Skinner and McLellan (1980) have proposed that the aerobic threshold is the point where fast twitch fibres are first recruited, resulting in an increase in blood lactate.

Anaerobic Threshold

Anaerobic threshold has been given many definitions. Heck et al. (1985) have defined threshold as the exercise intensity where blood lactate values reach 4mMol. Stegmann, Kindermann and Schnabel (1981) have developed a mathematical formula for determining individual anaerobic thresholds. The first definition of anaerobic threshold was proposed by Wasserman et al. (1973) and was defined as the level of work or O_2 consumption just below that at which metabolic acidosis and the associated changes in gas exchange occur. Hughson, Weisiger, and Swanson (1987) suggest that there is no breakaway or threshold point but that lactate increases in a curvilinear function from the beginning of exercise, and that there is an exponential increase in energy production through the anaerobic pathways.

For the purposes of this book threshold will be considered a point around 4mMol where lactate accumulation in the blood is increasing by more than 1mMol (Thoden, 1991). It may be easiest to think of anaerobic threshold as the point where the athlete is producing lactic acid at a rate faster than they can get rid of it. This causes an accumulation of lactic acid in the body.

There is no one cause of anaerobic threshold. Several mechanisms have been proposed: Inadequate supply of oxygen to the muscle (Wasserman et al. 1973), progressive recruitment of larger motor units (Clausen, 1976), decreased lactate removal (Brooks, 1985), and increased catecholamine (adrenaline) release (Davies et al. 1974) all work together to create the effect called anaerobic threshold.

VO$_2$ max (maximal aerobic power; MAP)

Maximal aerobic power is one of the most commonly measured physiological variables. It is the best measure of the functional limits of the cardiovascular system (Rowell and Human, 1974) and is often used as a measure of physical fitness. VO_2 max is the maximum amount of oxygen that the body can take in and use. It is the amount of oxygen that can be consumed per unit of time during large muscle group activity that is of progressively increasing intensity until the subject reaches exhaustion (Thoden, 1991). There is a

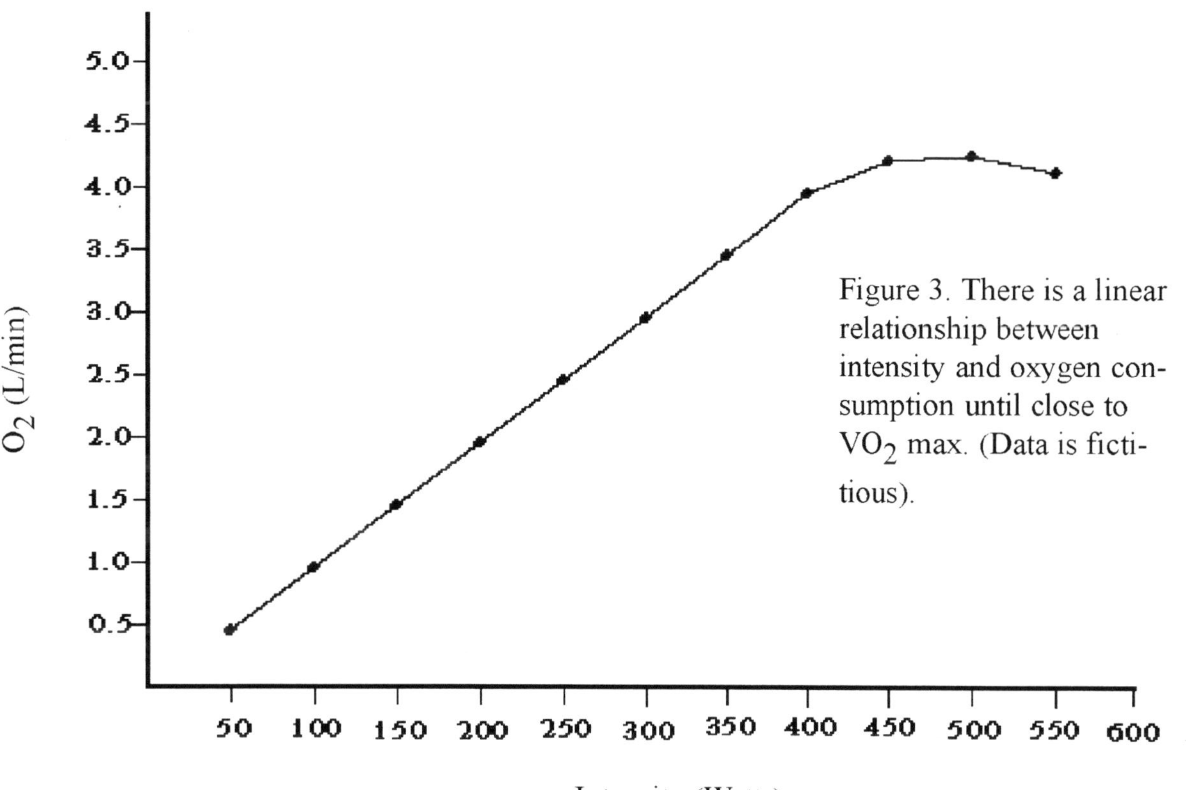

Figure 3. There is a linear relationship between intensity and oxygen consumption until close to VO_2 max. (Data is fictitious).

31

linear relationship between exercise intensity and oxygen consumption as seen in figure 3. (Howley, Bassett, and Welch, 1995).

MAP is dependant upon the integrated function of pulmonary ventilation, diffusion of oxygen from lungs to blood, cardiac output, redistribution of blood flow, and extraction and utilization of oxygen in the blood (ACSM, 1991).

It has been suggested that VO_2 max is related to rowing performance (Thoden, 1991, Kramer et al. 1994). If rowers of different levels are compared, those with the high VO_2 max scores will probably be the better performers. However, a poor relationship between VO_2 max and endurance performance is seen when people of similar VO_2 max values are compared (McLellan and Cheung, 1992). Anaerobic threshold tends to be a better indicator of performance in rowers of similar abilities.

The Training Categories

There are five different training categories within the aerobic system and one anaerobic category. Each category is designed to produce a specific adaptation. In a year-long training program, the categories would be performed in the order in which they are presented. For each of the categories an exercise prescription table is presented. This table should be used as a general guide only. Training programs should always be based on the fitness level of the individual even if that means starting below the recommended volumes and intensities.

Category VI

Category VI is the training category that represents all intensities up to and including the aerobic threshold. It is part of the training that many coaches and athletes call aerobic base training. Category VI training allows the coach to specifically target the slow twitch muscle fibres. In endurance sports, efficiency and proportion of slow twitch fibres are a limiting factor in performance (Larsson and Forsberg, 1980; Hagerman and Staron, 1983; Steinacker, 1993; Horowitz, Sidossis, and Coyle, 1994; Coyle et al. 1992; Fink, Costill, and Pollock, 1977; Rusko, Havu, and Karvinen, 1978). At relatively low speeds of movement slow twitch fibres are more efficient at converting chemical energy into mechanical work than fast twitch fibres (Horowitz, Sidossis, and Coyle, 1994).

Rowing races occur at an intensity much higher than category VI. Higher intensity interval training is needed to row fast. Since lactate is at least partially responsible for the fatigue associated with intense intermittent activities (Roberts and Smith, 1989; Tesch et al.,1978; Duchateau, Montigny, and Hainut ,1987; Horita and Ishiko, 1987) the ability to remove and metabolize lactate during rest periods is of prime importance. If the lactate is not removed, the athlete will not be able to maintain the speed or power of the next interval. If the speed decreases from interval to interval, the training adaptations are reduced. There is a relationship between the rate of lactate removal and the amount of slow twitch fibres (Bonen, et al. 1978). This relationship is based on the high content of H-LDH enzymes found in slow twitch fibres (this is an enzyme that is partially responsible for the metabolism of lactate), which has been found to increase with endurance training (Sjodin, Jacobs, and Svendenhag, 1982). Training in category VI allows the athlete to do more high-intensity interval work.

Training in category VI is typically long-duration, steady-state exercise (exercise done at a constant speed). Category VI is often used for technical training in endurance sports such as cycling and rowing. In these sports, category VI training may account for as much as 80% of the total training volume. Since the lactate levels in category VI are very low, fatigue will probably be the result of glycogen depletion, an imbalance of the ratio of tryptophan to branched chain amino acids (Blomstrand et al 1989, 1991; Blomstrand, Hassmen,

Table 1. Exercise Prescription Guidelines
for Category VI

Cat. VI	
Time/Session	45 min-2 hours
Sessions /Week	3-8
Sessions/Day	1-3
Style	Continuous steady state
Maintenance	2-3/wk

and Newsholme, 1991; Newsholme et al., 1991), body temperature, or soft-tissue trauma (Thoden, 1991).

Since category VI encompasses a wide range of intensities there is also significant variation in the volume of training that is done per training session.

When designing exercise prescriptions for category VI several key concepts should be remembered. (1) Long training sessions are done less frequently. For example, four-hour training sessions need only be done three to four times per week but 60 minute sessions may be done eight to 10 times per week. (2) The duration of the training session should, in part, be based on the demands of the event. In a sports such as football, where there are long rest periods and alternation between offensive and defensive players, 45-minute training sessions would be more appropriate than two-hour training sessions. (3) During certain phases of the year training will be focused on specific event preparation. During this time category VI training should be maintained so that detraining does not occur. (4) Maintenance refers to the number of sessions per week that need to be done to prevent detraining. (5) If the training session is less than two hours long another category VI session could be done with two to four hours rest.

Category V

Category V represents those training intensities between aerobic threshold and anaerobic threshold. Category V is part of aerobic base training. Since category V is between the thresholds the lactate values for this category fall between two and 4 mMol of lactate. Sjodin and Jacobs (1981) found that marathon running is done at a velocity that is about 87% of anaerobic threshold. Kumagai et al (1982) found that, in comparing five-km, 10-km, and 10-mile running races, the shorter the race the better the correlation to speed at anaerobic threshold. The results of these studies suggest that very long distance racing, seen in some head races, is done in category V.

Category V training uses ST fibres as well as some FOG (fast oxidative glycolytic) fibres. FOG fibres are an endurance fast twitch fibre with as much or more aerobic capacity than slow twitch fibres (Baldwin et al. 1972). In rowers, the FOG fibres are the largest fibres but are not as plentiful as the slow twitch fibres (Larsson and Forsberg, 1980).

Training in category V can either be done as steady-state exercise or long undulating intervals. Since category V intervals are below anaerobic threshold they do not cause an accumulation of lactic acid.

Table 2. Exercise Prescription Guidelines for
Category V

Cat. V	
Time/Session	45 min-2 hours
Sessions /Week	2-5
Sessions/Day	1-3
Style	Continuous steady state
Maintenance	2-3/wk

Therefore, there are no set work and rest periods. The main purpose
of the intervals is to vary the motor units that are recruited by changing exercise intensity. Since the intensity is only slightly higher
training volumes tend to be similar to Category VI.

Category V training is usually started after two to three weeks of
category VI training are completed. The key concepts outlined in
category VI apply to category V. Category V sessions rely primarily
on carbohydrate as an energy source. The time between category V
sessions should be eight to 12 hours. When category V training is
started there may be a reduction in the number of category VI ses-

sions.

Category IV

Category IV represents a narrow category around anaerobic threshold. Typically, lactate values for this category will fall between about 3.5 and 5 mMol.

For activities that are continuous in nature and last more than five minutes anaerobic threshold is a better indicator of performance than VO₂ max (Heck et al. 1985). Astrand and Rodahl (1970) showed that, in a training program lasting several months, even though MAP did not change endurance capacity continued to increase. Farrell et al. (1979) and Kumagai et al. (1982) examined running performance of various distances and found a greater correlation between run performance and velocity at anaerobic threshold than at VO₂ max. Rhodes and McKenzie (1984) found a high correlation between actual marathon time and that predicted from the threshold measurements. The subjects were tested to find the running velocity at which they reached threshold. This running speed was used to predict the time they would run the 26-mile race. The competitors who performed the best had somewhat high VO₂ max scores, but more importantly had threshold levels that were at a high percentage of the VO₂ max values. Sjodin and Jacobs (1981) found a very high correlation ($r = 0.96$) for marathon running velocity and running velocity at anaerobic threshold.These finding have been supported by Tanaka et al. (1984) who concluded that a close relationship exists between running velocity corresponding to race pace and that which corresponded to threshold.

Steinacker (1993) has stated that endurance capacity measured as the power which elicits a blood lactate level of 4 mMol is the most predictive parameter for competition performance in trained rowers, especially in the small boats. In Canadian National Team rowers, we

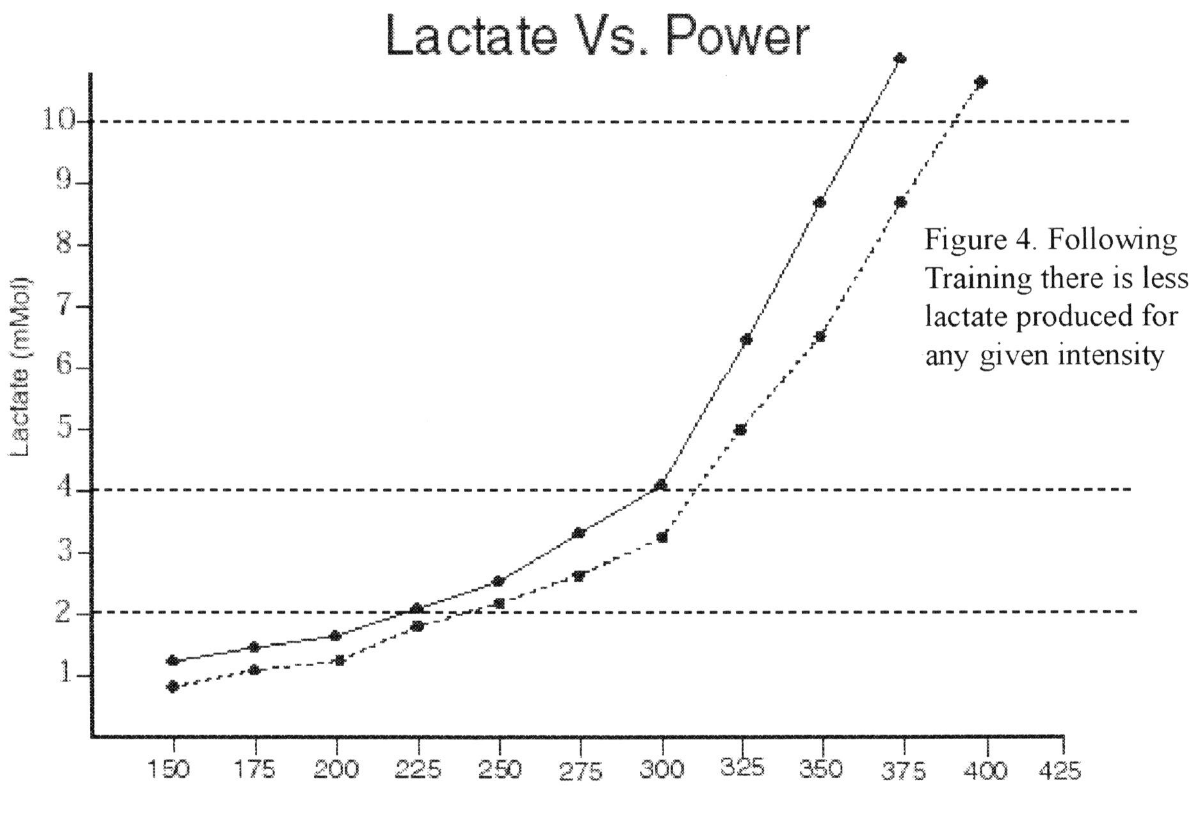

Figure 4. Following Training there is less lactate produced for any given intensity

have seen very high correlations (r = 0.93) between anaerobic threshold power output and 2000m ergometer performance. Recently, an analysis of data revealed the average wattage at anaerobic threshold was a good predictor of who rowed in the priority boat following national team time trials for lightweight men.

Training to Increase Threshold

When training anaerobic threshold the main objectives are to raise the workload at which threshold occurs and to improve endurance capacity at threshold. Two approaches have been used to raise threshold, continuous intensity training and intermittent type training. Continuous training approaches have typically involved exercising for an extended period at or below threshold. Intermittent approaches have gone above and below threshold in an alternating fashion. Both approaches appear to be successful in improving both absolute and relative threshold.

Poole (1985) tested the effects of 55 min continuous exercise at 50% MAP, 35 minutes at 70% MAP, and 10x2min intervals at 105% MAP. All three approaches increased threshold and no significant difference was found between groups. Coen and Scharz (1991) tested various modes of training as well as various conditions including an endurance run on a flat terrain, a graded terrain and 5x1000m runs. They concluded that training for threshold should be done in the range of 85 to 92% of threshold if the training is to be done over an extended period. This will prevent any possibility of overtraining. Training that is performed at nearly 100% of threshold will result in a significant amount of sympathetic nervous system activity, an outcome the authors believe will make it difficult to perform this activity on a frequent basis. A study that tested the effects of training at above, and below anaerobic threshold (Keith et al., 1992) found there was no statistical difference between training groups. It did, however, conclude that the mean intensity during training determines the extent of the adaptation. Figure 4 shows the relationship between lactate and power output before and after training. For any

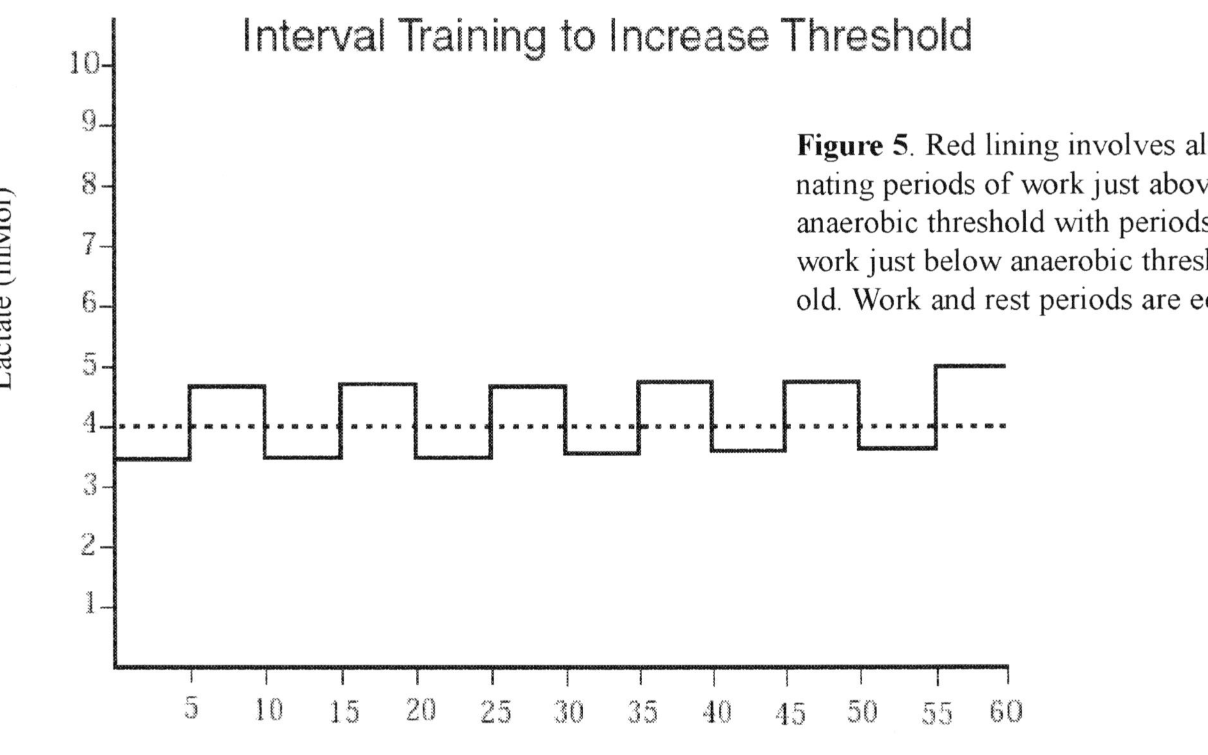

Figure 5. Red lining involves alternating periods of work just above anaerobic threshold with periods of work just below anaerobic threshold. Work and rest periods are equal

Table 3. Exercise Prescription Guidelines
for Category IV

Cat. IV	
Time/Session	30-90 min
Sessions /Week	1-5
Sessions/Day	1-2

Style
    work time
    rest time
	Interval or Steady state
	5-10 min
	5-10 min

Maintenance	2-3/wk

lactate level, including both aerobic and anaerobic threshold, more work is done after training.

One form of interval training successfully used with many athletes on the Canadian National Team has been termed "red lining" by Dr. A.T. Reed from the University of Ottawa. In "red lining" periods of work 5 to 10% above threshold are alternated with recovery periods 5 to 10% below threshold (figure 5). This form of training allows a high volume of work to be done at an intensity just above anaerobic threshold. Training above threshold in this manner may result in a shift in fast twitch fibres from glycolytic to a more oxidative state.

Andersen and Henriksson (1977) found that untrained subjects exercising at 81% of MAP for eight weeks increased their proportion of FOG fibres by 10%.

Work to rest period for "red lining" are approximately equal and range between five and ten minutes. The rest interval is active rest just below anaerobic threshold near the top of category V.

Increasing Endurance Capacity

There can be great differences in the amount of time an individual can work at anaerobic threshold. This may be due to the number of different methods used to determine threshold, and is also likely due to fitness. Using a fixed threshold of 4mMol Mongoni, Sirtori, Lorenzelli, and Ceretelli (1990) found only eight of their 34 subjects were able to complete 60 minutes of exercise. The average work time for the others was 38.2 minutes. Denis et al (1982) exercised subjects at 86% of VO_2 max and found that although the workload was slightly above threshold, they were able to complete 60 minutes of exercise. Oyono-Enguelle et al. (1990) found subjects only able to complete 23.5 minutes of exercise at a 4mMol threshold. Orok et al. (1989) found that a workload equal to or slightly greater than an individual anaerobic threshold (IAT) resulted in work times ranging from three to 36 minutes. It would seem safe to say that endurance capacity at anaerobic threshold is approximately 30 minutes.

Training to improve endurance capacity at anaerobic threshold is usually accomplished by steady-state training at or slightly above threshold. For this training, maintaining speed is very important. Heart rate is not always stable during training near threshold (Jacobs and McLellan, 1988) and may give a false indicator of the speed that should be used.

Category III

Category III represents intensities between anaerobic threshold and

Table 4. Exercise Prescription Guidelines
for Category III

Cat. III	
Time/Session	30-90 min
Sessions /Week	1-3
Sessions/Day	1

Style
    work time
    rest time
	Interval
	4-10 min
	8-20 min

Maintenance	1/wk

VO_2 max. Since category III is above anaerobic threshold training
has to be done interval style to obtain an adequate volume. One of
the objectives of category III training is to let the athlete perform at
higher levels of lactate and to promote lactate recovery. Many of
the cardiac adaptations to aerobic training are seen at this training
category. Since the intensity of category III training is quite high no
more than three training sessions per week of this training should be
scheduled. A 1996 study by Lindsay et al., using two interval session
per week at 86% of VO_2 max, found that peak power output and
time trial performance had improved by 5% and 3% following three

weeks of training. The increases from three to six weeks were insignificant suggesting that category III training does not have to be done for a long period of time to improve performance. Normally, category III is trained during the pre-competitive and competitive phases of the year with occasional maintenance sessions (once a month) during the rest of the year. The increase in peak power output following category III training is a good indicator of increased VO_2 max. Category III intervals are four to 10 minutes duration with eight to 20 minutes recovery. Recovery is active and is done in category VI. This is repeated for a total of 20 to 30 minutes of work time per training session.

Category II

Category II exercise is exercise in which the participants perform for as long as possible at VO_2 max. The objective of category II training is to increase VO_2 max and endurance time at VO_2 max. VO_2 max level exercise can normally be maintained for two to 12 minutes with an average of six minutes (Billat and Korzalstein, 1996). Some researchers have suggested that VO_2 max is of great importance to rowers. Secher et al. (1982) found that average VO_2 max of a crew was correlated to their results at the World Championships. A study like this can lead to some misinterpretation of the aerobic requirements of rowing. The importance of a high VO_2 max to rowing is probably not because of its impact on performance rather a high VO_2 max allows the athlete to have a higher anaerobic threshold. The VO_2 value at 4mMol is normally 85% of VO_2 max for trained rowers (Steinacker, 1993). In order to maintain this relationship and have anaerobic threshold move to a higher power output, VO_2 max must be increased. Figure 6 shows the changing relationship between VO_2 and anaerobic threshold.

Training in category II is similar to category III. Intervals consist of two to seven minutes work followed by 10 to 20 minutes rest. This

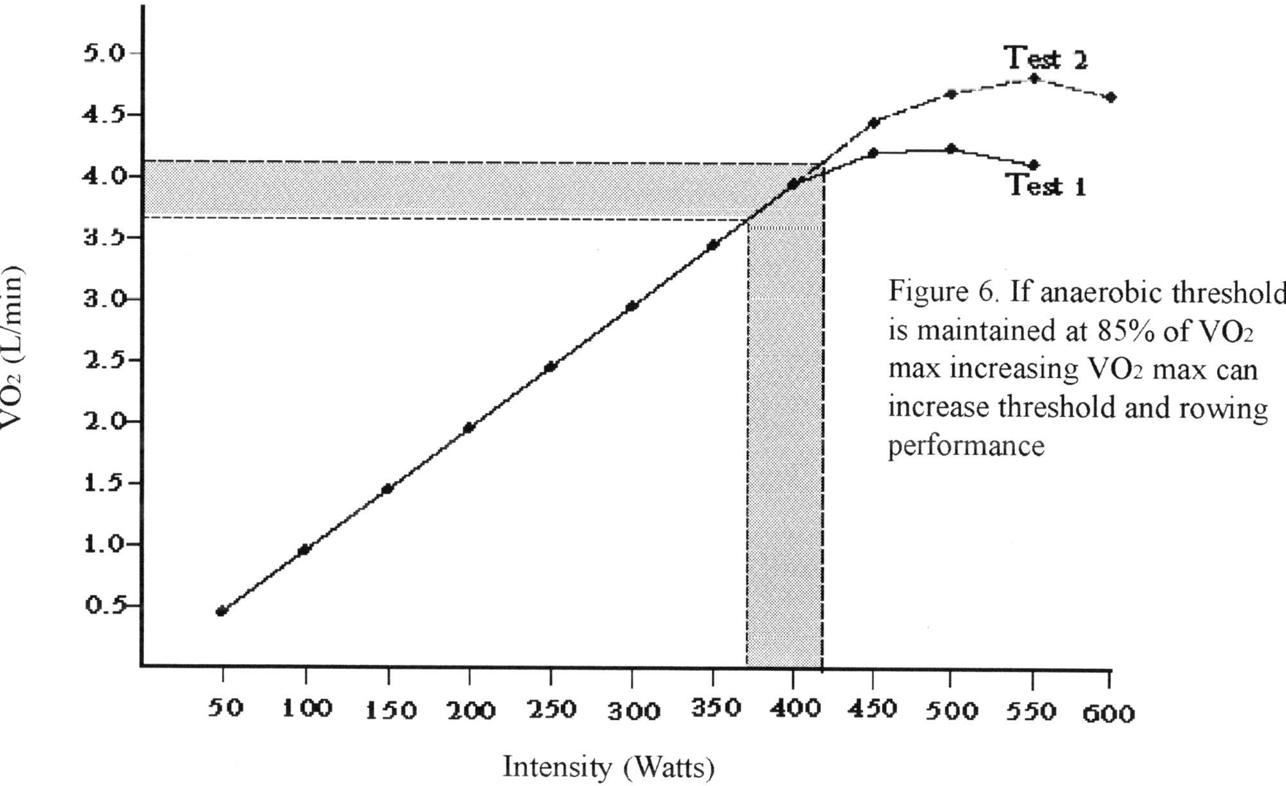

Figure 6. If anaerobic threshold is maintained at 85% of VO$_2$ max increasing VO$_2$ max can increase threshold and rowing performance

Table 4. Exercise Prescription Guidelines
for Category II

Cat. II	
Time/Session	30-90 min
Sessions /Week	1-2
Sessions/Day	1

Style
   work time
   rest time
	Interval
	2-7 min
	10-20 min

Maintenance	racing

is repeated for a total of 10 to 20 minutes of work per training session. Since the intensity is very high this type of training should only be done one to two times per week and only during the final part of the pre-competitive phase. Regular racing is often enough to maintain and even improve category II fitness.

Conclusion

Aerobic training can be done over a wide range of intensities. To break down this range, training category systems have been developed. Training category systems are based on three physiological points aerobic threshold, anaerobic threshold, and VO2 max. They allow coaches and athletes to create specific training adaptations and target selected muscle fibre types during training. Accurate determination of each of the five aerobic categories takes much of the guess work out of training program design.

References

Anderson, G.S. Rhodes, E.C. A review of blood lactate and ventilatory methods of detecting transition thresholds. Sports Medicine 8(1): 43-55, 1989.

Andersen, P., and Henriksson, J. (1977). Training induced changes in the subgroups of human type II skeletal muscle fibres. Acta Physiol. Scand. 99: 123-125.

Antonutto, G., and DiPrampero, P. (1995). The concept of lactate threshold. J. Sports Med. Phys. Fitness. 35: 6-12.

Astrand, P., and Rodahl, K. (1970). Textbook of Work Physiology. McGraw-Hill. NY, NY.

Aunola, S. Rusko, H. Aerobic and anaerobic thresholds determined from venous lactate or from ventilation and gas exchange in relation to muscle fiber composition. Intl J Sports Med. (7) 161-166. (1986).

Aunola, S. Marniemi, J. Muscle metabolic profile and oxygen transport capacity as determinants of aerobic and anaerobic thresholds. Eur J Appl Physiol. 57: 726-734. (1988).

Aunola, S. and Rusko, H.(1986) Aerobic and anaerobic thresholds determined from venous lactate or from ventilation and gas exchange in relation to muscle fiber composition. Intl J Sports Med. (7) 161-166.

Baldwin, K., Klinkerfuss, G., Terjung, R., Mole, P., and Holloszy, J. (1972). Respiratory capacity of white, red, and intermediate muscle: Adaptive response to exercise. Am. J. Physiol. 222: 373-378.

Beaver, William L. Wasserman, Karlman. Bicarbonate buffering of lactic acid generated during exercise. J Appl. Physiol. 60(2): 472-478. (1986)

Beaver, W., Wasserman, K., and Whipp, B. (1986). A new method for detecting anaerobic threshold by gas exchange. J. Appl. Physiol. 60(6): 2020-2027.

Blomstrand, E., Hassmen, P., Newsholme, E. (1991). Effects of branch chain amino acid supplementation on mental performance. Acta Physiol. Scand. 143: 225-226

Blomstrand, E., Hassmen, P., Ekblom, B., and Newsholme, E. (1991). Administration of branched chain amino acids during exercise- effects on performance and on plasma concentration of amino acids. Eur. J. Appl. Physiol. 63: 83-88.

Blomstrand, E., Perret, D., Parry-Billings, M., and Newsholme, E. (1989). Effect of sustained exercise on plasma amino acid concentrations and on 5-HT metabolism in six different brain regions in the rat. Acta Physiol. Scand. 136: 473-481.

Bonen, A., Campbell, C., Kirby, R., and Belcastro, A. (1978). Relationship between slow twitch muscle fibres and lactic acid removal. Can. J. Appl. Sport Sci. 3(3): 160-162.

Brooks, G. A. (1985). Anaerobic Threshold: review of the concept and directions for future research. Medicine and Science in Sports and Exercise. 17: 22-31.

Brooks, G. A. (1986). The lactate shuttle during exercise and recovery . Medicine and Science in Sports and Exercise. 18(3): 360-368.

Burke, R. (1986). The control of muscle force: motor unit recruitment and firing patterns. In Human Muscle Power Jones, McCartney, and McComas (eds). Human Kinetics. Champagne, Ill.

Brooks, George A. Anaerobic Threshold: review of the concept and directions for future research. Medicine and Science in Sports and Exercise. 17: 22-31. (1985).

Bulbulian, Ronald. Wilcox, Anthoney. Anaerobic contribution to distance running performance of trained cross- country athletes. Medicine and Science in Sports and Exercise. 18: 107-113. (1986).

Caiozzo, Vincent J. Davis, James A. A comparison of gas exchange methods used to detect the anaerobic threshold. J Appl. Physiol. 53(5): 1184-1189. (1982).

Chwalbinska-Moneta, Jolanta. Robergs, Robert A. Threshold for muscle lactate accumulation during progressive exercise. J Appl. Physiol. 66(6): 2710-2716. (1989).

Clausen, J. (1976). Circulatory adjustments to dynamic exercise and effect of physical training in normal subjects and in patients with coronary artery disease. Prog. Cardiovascular Diseases. 18: 459-495

Coen, B. Scharz, L. Control of training in Middle and Long Distance Running by means of the individual anaerobic threshold. Intl J Sports Medicine. 12:519-524. (1991).

Coyle, Edward F. Coggan, Andrew R. Determinants of endurance in well trained cyclists. J Appl Physiol. 64 (6): 2622-2630. (1988).

Coen, B. and Scharz, L. (1991). Control of training in Middle and Long Distance Running by means of the individual anaerobic threshold. Intl J Sports Medicine. 12:519-524.

Coyle, E., Sodissis, L., Horowitz, J., and Beltz, J. (1992). Cycling efficiency is related to the percentage of type I muscle fibers. Med. Sci. Sports Exerc. 24: 782-788.

Davis, James A. Frank, Marianne H. Anaerobic threshold alterations caused by endurance training in middle aged men. J Appl Physiol. 46 (6): 1039-1046. (1979)

Davis, James A. Anaerobic Threshold: review of the concept and directions for future research. Medicine and Science in Sports and Exercise. 17:6-18. (1985).

Davies, C., Foster, K., and Sargeant, A. (1974). Plasma cate-cholamine concentration during dynamic exercise involving different muscle groups. Eur. J. Appl. Physiol. 32: 195-206.

Davis, J. (1985). Anaerobic Threshold: review of the concept and directions for future research. Medicine and Science in Sports and Exercise. 17:6-18.

Denis, C. Fouquet, R., Poty, P., Geyssant, A., and Lacour, J. (1982). Effect of 40 weeks of endurance training on the anaerobic threshold. Intl J Sports Med. 3(4):208-214.

Denis, C. Fouquet, R. Effect of 40 weeks of endurance training on the anaerobic threshold. Intl J Sports Med. 3(4):208-214. (1982).

Duchateau, J., Montigny, L., and Hainaut, K. (1987). Electro mechanical failures and lactate production during fatigue. Eur. J.

Apple Physiol. 56: 287-291.

Eddy, Duane O. Sparks, Kenneth L. The effects of continuous and interval training in women and men. Eur J Appl Physiol. 37: 83-92. (1977).

Farrell, Peter A. Wilmore, Jack H. Plasma lactate accumulation and distance running performance. Medicine and Science in Sports and Exercise. 11: 338-344. (1979).

Farrell, P. Wilmore, J. et al. (1979). Plasma lactate accumulation and distance running performance. Medicine and Science in Sports and Exercise. 11: 338-344.

Fink, W., Costill, D., and Pollock, M. (1977). Submaximal and maximal working capacity of elite distance runners. Part II. Muscle fibre composition and enzyme activity. Ann. NY. Acad. Sci. 301: 323-327.

Fohrenbach, R. Mader. A. Determination of endurance capacity and prediction of exercise intensities for training and competition in marathon runners. Intl J Sports Med. 8:11-18. (1987).

Gaessar, G.A.. Poole, D.C. Dissociation between Vo2max and ventilatory threshold responses to endurance training. Eur J Appl Physiol. 53: 242-247. (1984).

Gaessar, Glenn A. Poole, David C. Lactate and ventilatory thresholds: disparity in time course of adaptations to training. J Appl Physiol. 61 (3): 999-1004. (1986).

Gaessar, G.A. Wilson, L.A. Effects of continuous and interval training on the parameters of the power endurance time relationship for high intensity exercise. Intl J Sports Med. 9(6): 417-421. (1988).

Green, H.J. Hughson, R.L. Anaerobic threshold, blood lactate, and muscle metabolites in progressive exercise. J Appl Physiol. 54 (4): 1032-1038. (1983).

Guidelines for Exercise Testing and Prescription. ACSM. Lea and Febiger: Philadelphia.PA. 1991

Hagerman, F.C., and Staron, R.S. (1983). Seasonal variations among physiological variables in elite oarsmen. Can. J. Appl. Spt. Sci. 8(3): 143-148.

Heck, H., Mader, A., Hess, G., Mucke, S., Muller, R., and Hollmann, W. (1985). Justification of the 4mmol/L lactate threshold. Intl J Sports Med. 6:117-130.

Henneman, E. (1957). Relation between size of neurons and their susceptibility to discharge. Science. 126: 1345-1347.

Horita, T., and Ishiko, T. (1987). Relationship between muscle lactate accumulation and surface EMG activities during isokinetic contractions in man. Eur. J. Appl. Physiol. 56: 18-23.

Horowitz, J., Sidossis, L., and Coyle, E. (1994). High efficiency of type I muscle fibres improves performance. Int. J. Sports. Med. 15(3): 152-157.

Howley, E., Bassett, D., and Welch, H. (1995). Criteria for maximal oxygen uptake: review and commentary. Med. Sci. Sports. Exerc. 27(9): 129-1301.

Hughson, R., Weisiger, K., and Swanson, G. (1987). Blood lactate concentration increases as a continuous function in progressive exercise. J. Appl. Physiol. 62: 1975-1981.

Hughes, Ellen F. Turner, Sue. Effects of glycogen depletion and pedalling speed on the anaerobic threshold. J Appl Physiol. 52(6): 1598-

1607. (1982).

Hurley, Ben F. Magberg, James M. Effects of training on blood lactate levels during submaximal exercise. J Appl Physiol. 56(5):1260-1264. (1984).

Ivy, J.L. Withers, R.T. Muscle respiratory capacity and fiber type as determinants of the lactate threshold. J Appl Physiol. 48(3):523-527. (1980).

Jacobs, I and McLellan, T. (1988). Validity of the individual anaerobic threshold (IAT). Can. J. Sport Sci. 13: 60p

Keith, S., Jacobs, I., and McLellan, T. (1992). Adaptations to training at the individual anaerobic threshold. Eur J Appl Physiol. 65:316-323.

Kindermann, W., Simon, G., and Keul, J., The significance of the aerobic-anaerobic transition for determination of workload intensities during endurance training. Eur. J. Appl. Physiol. 42: 25-34.

Kumagai, S., Tanaka, K., Matsuura, Y., Matsuzaka, A., Hirakoba, K., and Asano, K. (1982) Relationships of the anaerobic threshold with the 5km, 10km, and 10 mile races. Eur J Appl Physiol. 49:13-23.

Larsson, L and Forsberg, A (1980). Morphological Muscle Characteristic in Rowers. Can. J. Appl. Spt. Sci. 5(4): 239-244.

MacDougall, J.D. The anaerobic threshold: its significance for the endurance athlete. Can J Appl Sports Sci. 2:137-140. (1977).

Mader, A. Heck, H. A theory of the metabolic origin of anaerobic threshold. Intl J Sports Med. 7:45S-65S. (1986).

McLellan, T.M. Skinner, J.S. The use of the aerobic threshold as a basis for training. Can J Appl Sp Sci. 6:197-201. (1981).

McLellan, Tom.M. Jacbs, Ira. Active recovery, endurance training, and the calculation of the individual anaerobic threshold. Medicine and Science in Sports and Exercise. 21(5): 586-592. (1989).

McLellan, Tom M. Cheung, Kenneth. A comparative evaluation of the individual anaerobic threshold and the critical power. Medicine and Science in Sports and Exercise. 24(5): 543-550. (1992).

McLellan, T., Cheung, M., and Kenneth. (1992). A comparative evaluation of the individual anaerobic threshold and the critical power. Medicine and Science in Sports and Exercise. 24(5): 543-550.

Mognoni, P. Sirtori, M., Lorenzelli, F., and Ceretelli, P. (1990). Physiological responses during prolonged exercise at the power output corresponding to the blood lactate threshold. Eur J Appl. Physiol. 60:239-243.

Newsholme, E., Parry-Billings, M., McAndrew, N., and Budgett, R. (1991). A biochemical mechanism to explain some characteristics of overtraining. In Brouns (ed) Medical Sport Science, Vol. 32, Advance in nutrition and top sport. Karger, Basel.

Orok, C., Hughson, R., Green, H., and Thomson, J. (1989). Blood lactate response in incremental exercise as a predictor of constant load performance. Eur. J. Appl. Physiol. 59: 262-267.

Orr, G., Green, H., Hughson, R., and Bennett, G. (1982). A computer linear regression model to determine ventilatory anaerobic threshold. J. Appl. Physiol. 52(5): 1349-1352

Oyono-Enguelle, S., Heitz, A., et al. (1990). Blood lactate during constant load exercise at aerobic and anaerobic thresholds. Eur. J. Appl. Physiol. 60: 321-330.

Poole, D. and Gaessar, G. (1985). Response of ventilatory and lactate thresholds to continuous and interval training. J Appl Physiol. 58(4): 115-1121.

Ready, Elizabeth A. Quinney , H Arthur. Alterations in anaerobic threshold as a result of endurance training and detraining. Medicine and Science in Sports and Exercise. 14(4): 292-296. (1982).

Rhodes, E. and McKenzie, D (1984). Predicting marathon time from anaerobic threshold measurements. The Physician and Sports medicine. 12(1): 95-98.

Roberts, D., and Smith, D.J. (1989). Biochemical aspects of peripheral muscle fatigue. Sports Med. 7: 125-138.

Rowell, L., and Human, B. (1974). Human cardiovascular adjustments to exercise and thermal stress. Physiol. Rev. 54: 75-103.

Rusko, H., Havu, M., and Karvinen, E. (1978). Aerobic performance capacity in athletes. Eur. J. Appl. Physiol. 38: 151-159.

Sjodin, B. and Jacobs, I. (1981) Onset of blood lactate accumulation and marathon running performance. Intl J Sports Med. 2(1): 23-26.

Sjodin, B., Jacobs, I., and Svendenhag, J. (1982). Changes in onset of blood lactate accumulation (OBLA) and muscle enzymes after training at OBLA. Eur. J. Appl. Physiol. 49: 45-57.

Skinner, J., and McLellan, T. (1980). The transition from aerobic to anaerobic metabolism. Res. Quarterly. 51(1): 234-248.

Stegmann, H., Kindermann., and Schnabel, A. (1981). Lactate kinetics and individual anaerobic threshold. Int. J. Sports Med. 2: 160-165.

Stegmann, H. Kindermann, W. Comparison of prolonged exercise tests at the individual anaerobic threshold and the fixed anaerobic threshold of 4mmol/L lactate. Intl J Sports Med. 3: 105-110. (1982).

Steinacker, J.M. (1993). Physiological aspects of training for rowing. Int. J. Sports Med. 14(suppl1):S3-S10.

Tanaka, K., Matsuura, Y., et al. (1984). Marathon performance, anaerobic threshold, and onset of blood lactate accumulation.

Tesch, P.A. Sharp, D.S. Influence of fiber type composition and capillary density on onset of blood lactate accumulation. Intl J Sports Medicine. 2(4): 252-255. (1981).

Thoden, J.S. Aerobic Power in Physiological Testing of the High Performance Athlete. Human Kinetics Publishers. (1991)

Withers, R.T. Sherman, W.M. Specificity of the anaerobic threshold in endurance trained cyclists and runners. Eur J Appl Physiol. 47: 93-104. (1981).

Yoshida, Takayoshi. Effect of exercise duration during incremental exercise on the determination of anaerobic threshold and the onset of blood lactate accumulation. Eur J Appl Physiol. 53: 196-199. (1984).

Yoshida, Takayoshi. Effect of dietary modifications on lactate threshold and onset of blood lactate accumulation during incremental exercise. Eur J Appl Physiol. 53: 200-205. (1988)

Determining Aerobic Training Categories

3

The concept of aerobic training categories is only of value if the categories are determined individually for the athlete. Many coaches try to prescribe the same heart rate or wattage range for every athlete without consideration for variations in fitness level or physiological differences. This is often done because the coaches don't have the tools or knowledge to determine the categories.

Methods of Determining Training Categories

There are two methods that can be used to determine aerobic training categories. (1) Direct measures involving either gas exchange or blood lactate measures and (2) prediction methods involving the prediction of training categories based on various performance tests. Direct measures are by far the most accurate way to determine the categories but they can be expensive and are not always readily available to individuals or clubs not linked to colleges with human performance laboratories.

Direct Measures

Blood Lactate Analysis

With the advent of affordable portable lactate analyzers and mail-order analysis labs, lactate analysis has grown in popularity. Since the training categories have been developed based on lactate levels this is also potentially the most accurate method of intensity determination. Thoden (1991) has proposed several characteristics of lactate tests:

- Use a mode of exercise specific to the competitive

performance. In other words, rowers need to be tested on the water or on an ergometer. The training zones developed from a bike or treadmill test can't be used for rowing. Conversely, the categories from a rowing-specific test can't be used for running or biking.

- Set the workload at or above 30% of VO_2 max. This represents an intensity that is about 30% of 2000m pace. Starting intensities lower than this are so low that most rowers will not be able to effectively row that easily and results will be artificially high.

- Employ work-load increments of at least two minute duration. The lactate response to an increase in intensity can be seen in figure 1. The longer the stage the greater the confidence reach ingthe stable part of the curve. Different countries use different durations of stages during their lactate testing. Typically, stages will vary from three to five minutes induration but stages of up to eight minutes have been tried in several countries. The differ ences in time to achieve a lactate steady state may in part be due to the difference in whole blood or plasma analysis techniques. Typically, plasma lactate will require longer stages to reach an equilibrium point.

- Employ fingertip or earlobe sites for direct sampling of capillary blood. There may be some differences in lactate levels due to sampling site. The most important factor is consistency. Every test should employ the same sampling technique.

- Results should be reported in terms of the individual's response to exercise. Thresholds and training categories should be developed using both heart rate and wattage (split time) ranges.

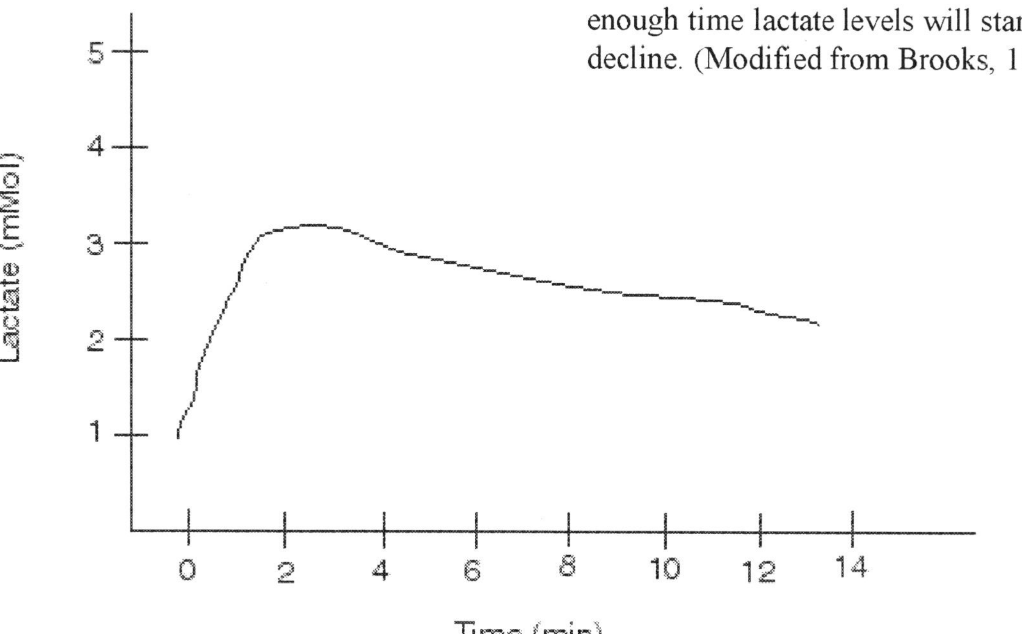

Figure 1. Lactate response over time for steady state exercise After an initial rapid increase in lactate there is a plateau. Given enough time lactate levels will start to decline. (Modified from Brooks, 1991)

Pre-Test Procedure

The training and nutritional regimens two days prior to the testing session can have an impact on the results. The following guidelines should be followed prior to each testing session. This will help ensure accuracy in test administration and data interpretation.

- Maintain a high-carbohydrate diet

Try to emphasize foods such as pasta, rice, bread, and potatoes in your meals. Some type of carbohydrate drink (gatorade, power ade, exceed, etc.) should be consumed immediately (within 30 minutes) following your workouts. Fat and protein will have no effect on lactate levels, but may detract from the amount of carbohydrate consumed. Avoid all alcohol.

- Caffeine raises both lactate and heart rate levels

Do not consume caffeinated beverages in the 90-minute period before the test. If the athlete has a morning test and is a habitual caffeine user they should try to consume their caffeine early enough so that it will not affect the test results.

- Avoid higher intensity training

Strength training and categories V, IV, and III all use carbohydrates as their major fuel source. Carbohydrate depletion will result in false results. If the athlete is training in the two days prior to testing try to do only category VI, and technical sessions. Use some form of carbohydrate drink during these sessions and try to keep them to 90 minutes or less. Only one training session should be done the day before the test.

The Test

The test is a progressive, incremental, discontinuous, submaximal test. Each stage is three to five minutes long, wattages are increased each stage, the wattages used are determined by your category and gender (i.e. lightweight or heavyweight, male or female). One minute of rest is given between each stage during which lactate samples are taken from the finger tip or ear lobe.

Warm Up

The warm up should be standardized for each athlete and consistent from test to test. The warm up should be of sufficient duration to increase temperature but not so long as to decrease intramuscular glycogen levels. Ten to 15 minutes of rowing at an intensity slightly below or equal to the intensity of the first stage of the test is usually sufficient. Allow the athlete to have a drink of water before the test starts. There should be no more than 10 minutes between the end of the warm up and the start of the test.

Stroke Rate

There doesn't seem to be much consensus on the influence of stroke rate on test results. Some countries allow the athlete to choose a stroke rate that is comfortable to achieve a given wattage. In the Canadian system we have used a stroke rate that is held constant throughout the test and falls between 22 and 26 strokes per minute. More work needs to be done to determine how much of an effect stroke rate has on lactate levels

Test Performance

The average watt reading on the Concept II ergometer is used for this test so the athlete needs to be as consistent as possible during each stage. The athlete should build up to the desired wattage over the first 15 seconds of the stage. Some athletes will try to 'cheat' the test by using a racing start for the first few strokes and then sitting at a lower wattage for the rest of the stage.

Resistance

A variety of resistances (vent setting or drag factor on the Concept II) have been used in lactate testing. It is still unclear as to how much of an effect changing the resistance has on test results. Anecdotal evidence suggests that the lactates may be higher for any given wattage as the resistance increases but this still needs to be formally investigated.

Wattages

The wattage for each stage and the number of stages will depend on the level of the athlete and the finances available for the testing (more stages usually costs more). At least four stages are needed to develop a graph from which the training categories can be developed. If the number of stages have to be limited because of time or money constraints, it is more important to have stages below anaerobic threshold than above anaerobic threshold. This will allow the development of categories VI through IV which should comprise the majority of training time. Tables 1 to 3 provide some suggested wattages for various performance levels. These wattages are not the only possible ranges but have been found to provide lactate levels appropriate for the determination of all training categories.

As a final word of caution: Although the technology is available for coaches to perform a lactate analysis on their athletes, all lactate testing should be done by an experienced technician. There is a certain amount of skill involved in taking and analyzing blood samples. The athletes may lose confidence in the coach and the program if they are given results inconsistent with other indicators of their performance. There are also certain liability issues in the drawing and

Table 1. Suggested Test Wattages for National Level Athletes

Stage	HW Men	HW Women	LW Men	LW Women
1	260	160	190	140
2	295	190	230	170
3	330	220	270	200
4	365	250	310	230
5	400	280	350	260
6	435	310	390	290

Table 2. Suggested Test Wattages for College Level Athletes (NCAA Division II, III, Canadian Universities or equivalent)

Stage	HW Men	HW Women	LW Men	LW Women
1	185	125	150	100
2	215	155	180	130
3	245	185	210	160
4	275	215	240	190
5	305	245	270	220
6	335	275	300	250

Table 3. Suggested Test Wattages for Club Level Athletes

Stage	HW Men	HW Women	LW Men	LW Women
1	150	100	125	75
2	180	130	155	105
3	210	160	185	135
4	240	190	215	165
5	270	220	245	195
6	300	250	275	225

Note: The level of performance in club athletes can vary depending on experience and the competitive nature of the individual and club. These wattages should serve as a starting point but may have to be modified to accommodate higher level club competitors handling of blood samples which can be reduced by allowing a trained technician perform the tests.

Gas Exchange Methods

Gas exchange methods are a non-invasive alternative to lactate measures for determining anaerobic threshold (Davis et al, 1976; Reinhard et al, 1979; Wasserman and McIlroy, 1964; Anulo and Rusko, 1986). There are a number of methods that can be used to determine thresholds from gas exchange (Caiozzo et al. 1982). Combinations of VO_2, VCO_2, and VE are typically analyzed for changes in the linearity of the curves produced by exercise (figure 2).

There are advantages and disadvantages to using gas exchange over lactate. The cost is usually the same or slightly higher for gas exchange methods. Unlike lactate testing, where many people can do the test simultaneously, gas exchange tests can only be done on one person at a time, increasing the time it takes to test a crew. While there doesn't seem to be any difference in the anaerobic thresholds determined by gas or lactate, it is often difficult to find aerobic threshold from gas exchange tests. On the positive side, being non-invasive decreases the liability associated with gas testing. In addition, VO_2 max values can be obtained from this type of testing.

The use of gas measures to determine training zones based on lactate levels is questionable. Poole and Gasser (1985) have demonstrated that training affects ventilatory anaerobic threshold differently than lactate threshold. Simon et al. (1983) found that ventilatory anaerobic threshold peaked before plasma lactate peaked suggesting that ventilation does not increase proportionately with blood lactate. Differences in lactate and ventilatory thresholds have also been seen under conditions of glycogen depletion. Glycogen depleted athletes

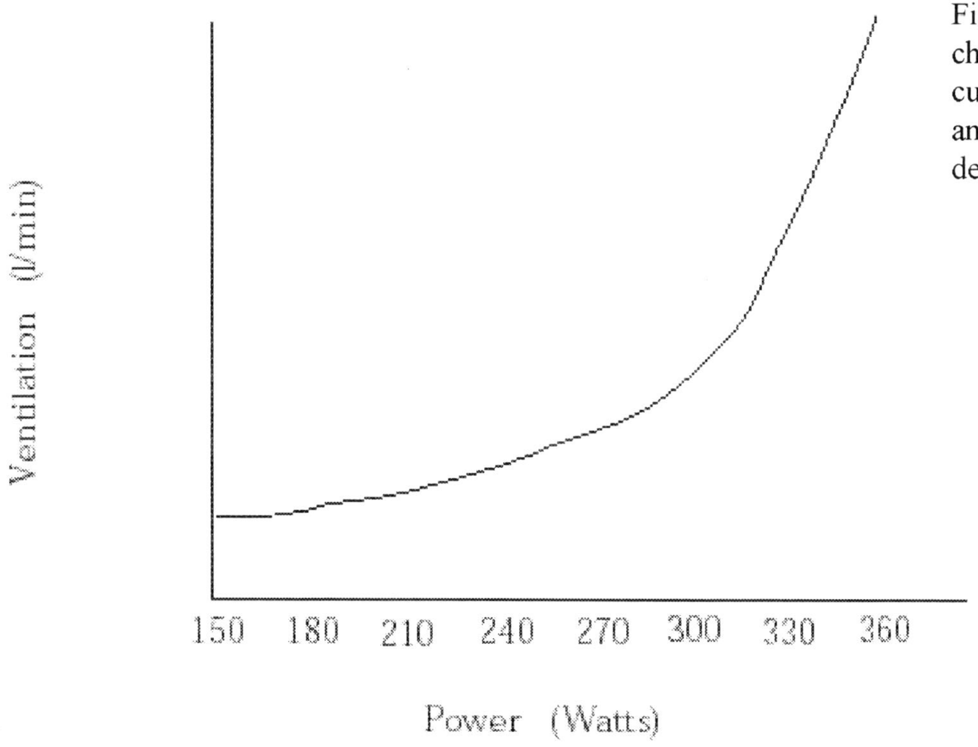

Figure 2: By analyzing changes in the ventilation curve (VE) aerobic and anaerobic threshold can be determined

cannot produce lactate (if there is no glycogen to burn anaerobically lactate production and power output are limited) but don't experience any difference in ventilatory threshold (Hughes et al., 1982). If gas exchange methods are used instead of lactate measures, keep in mind the interpretation of the data and training response may be very different between the two methods. Try to find a technician who has experience with both lactate and gas exchange methods to help determine the training categories and interpret the results.

Pre-test procedures and warm up and wattages for each stage are the same for gas exchange methods and lactate testing. The stage duration can be reduced to two to three minutes for gas-exchange testing.

Estimation of Training Categories

While direct measures are the best way of determining training categories they require special equipment and technicians to perform the tests. There are several ways of estimating training categories using data from field tests.

Conconi Method

The Conconi test was developed in 1982 as a non-invasive indirect determination of anaerobic threshold in runners (Conconi et al. 1982). Since then the Conconi test has been used on athletes in a variety of sports including rowing (Conconi et al. 1996). The test was based on an observation of a deflection point in the heart rate work intensity relationship (Bourgois and Vrijens, 1998). A detailed description of the protocol is published in the *International Journal of Sports Medicine*, Volume 17, pages 509-519.

There has been much criticism of the Conconi test. About half of the studies that have tried to replicate the results have failed to do so (Conconi et al. 1996). The reasons for this are unclear and may be

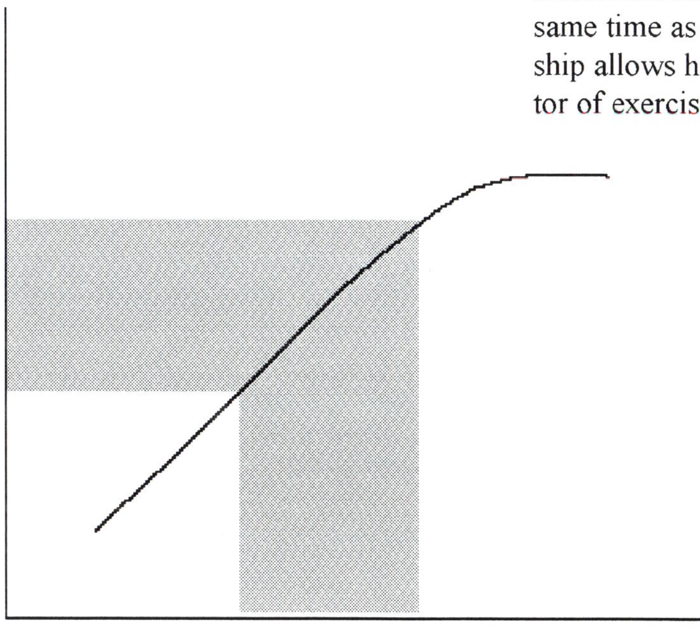

Figure 3: Linear Relationship Between Oxygen Consumption and Heart Rate. Maximum heart rate is achieved around the same time as VO2 max. This linear relationship allows heart rate to be used as an indicator of exercise intensity.

the result of improper test performance or data interpretation (Conconi, 1996). A recent study designed to strictly follow the guidelines for test performance set out by Conconi found there was an identifiable heart-rate deflection point for young rowers. This deflection point however did not correlate with anaerobic threshold determined either through gas exchange or lactate measures (Bourgois and Vrijens, 1998). These results are similar to those seen in other attempts to validate the Conconi test in rowing. Only the work of Droghetti et al. (1986) has been able to find a good correlation between heart rate deflection and anaerobic threshold in rowers.

Even if the reliability and validity of the Conconi test were not questionable it still would not be a good test for determining training categories. Since this test is designed only to find anaerobic threshold (power at VO2 max could also be determined with slight modifications to the protocol) it is impossible to determine categories VI or V. Since these categories comprise the majority of a rowers training volume this is a major limitation.

Maximal Heart Rate Methods

Many coaches rely on percentages of maximal heart rate as means of estimating thresholds and training zones.The use of heart rate to determine exercise intensity is possible because there is a relatively linear relationship between heart rate and oxygen consumption (Figure 3). This relationship exists for most continuous rhythmical exercises. However, the relationship, though linear, is not the same for all exercises. In other words using 70% of maximum heart rate for erging and treadmill running may induce different training responses. This makes the use of heart rate as the sole indicator of exercise intensity difficult when training for very specific adaptations such as those needed by athletes. However, since health adaptations can occur over a wide variety of exercise intensities heart rate can be used to set upper and lower limits of exercise intensity for recreational rowing.

Determination of Heart Rate

Before the discussion of heart rate and exercise intensity can be continued methods of measuring heart rate should be discussed. There are several acceptable methods for measuring heart rate, pulse palpation, ECG, stethoscope, and heart rate monitor, each has advantages and disadvantages.

Palpation

Palpation involves manually feeling for a pulse rate either at the wrist or at the neck. This is a simple technique with no cost. However, since heart rate is typically counted for six, 10, or 15 seconds and multiplied to a one minute value the amount of error can be quite high. In addition, at very high heart rates or while moving, it is difficult to get an accurate count. Palpation is an acceptable means of determining if someone is within a large heart rate range but is not a good way to find a narrow or precise heart rate range during exercise.

Stethoscope

Placing a stethoscope to the chest and counting the heart beats is an alternative to palpation. Again, the heart rate is normally counted for six to 15 seconds and multiplied to a one-minute value. The stethoscope shares the same problems and limitations as palpation.

ECG

An electrocardiograph measures the electrical activity of the heart during the different phases of a beat. The ECG is very accurate at all heart rates and can be used to indicate existing or potential cardiac abnormalities. While the accuracy and value of ECG is unquestionable, the expense and need to have a physician to interpret the readings make it impracticle for everyday use.

Heart-Rate Monitors

Heart-rate monitors that include a chest strap and a receiver, usually in the form of a watch, offer the same accuracy as an ECG. Monitors can cost between $100 to $500 depending on the features. Displays are normally updated every five seconds. If narrow heart-rate ranges or precise measurement is required a heart-rate monitor is the most economical tool.

Determining Heart Rate Ranges

Two methods are commonly used to determine heart rate ranges. The first method is to use fixed percentages of maximal heart rate. Rough averages for the heart rate percentages for the different categories can be seen in Table 4. This is the least accurate method of heart rate training and basically amounts to nothing more than a rough guess. This method may be acceptable for people in a learn to row program but will probably result in very poor estimates for more fit individuals.

The second method is called the heart rate reserve method. With this method percentages of the difference between maximum and resting heart rate are used to determine a heart rate range. It has been found that 60 to 80% of heart rate reserve is equal to 60 to 80% VO2 max. Wealso know that in untrained people anaerobic threshold (AT) occurs at about 70% VO2 max. In moderately trained people AT is approximately 80 to 85% VO2 max and in highly trained rowers AT will be 87 to 92% VO2 max. Aerobic threshold will fall between 50 to 60% of VO2 max for untrained, 60 to70% for moderately trained and 70 to 80% for highly trained individuals. The calculation of the heart rate range for category VI for a moderately trained athlete with maximum heart rate of 200 and resting heart rate of 72 is seen in Table 5.

Table 4: Estimated Percentages of Maximum Heart Rate for the Various Categories of Aerobic training

Category	% Max HR
VI	60-70
V	70-80
IV	80-90
III	90-100

Maximum Heart Rate

All of the methods presented for determining heart rate training zones are based on percentages of maximum oxygen consumption or maximum heart rate. Maximum heart rate can be determined in two ways. Maximum heart rate can be estimated using the formula (220-age). This formula is only an estimate of maximum heart rate and has an error range of plus or minus 13 beats per minute. This type of error may be acceptable when dealing with individuals who are training to improve health. When more specific goals are established maximum heart rate should be determined directly.

Maximum heart rate can be determined through a progressive incremental test as outlined in Figure 4. This test should only be performed on apparently healthy individuals or with a doctor's permission.

Heart rate methods are the simplest but least reliable and accurate ways of determining training categories. They don't take into account performance level or the physiological variables that create thresholds. Heart rate has several weaknesses that need to be consid-

Table 5: Hear Rate Reserve Method for Calculating Training Categories.

	Lower Limit	Upper Limit
Maximum HR	200	200
Resting HR	- 72	-72
	128	128
% Maximum HR	x.60	x.70
	77	90
Resting HR	+72	+ 72
Target HR	149	162

For this athlete Cat VI falls between 149-162 bpm

ered before it can be used as a tool in monitoring training intensity.

Even though there is a relationship between exercise intensity and heart rate this relationship is different for different exercises, i.e. heart rates for running will not be the same as heart rates for rowing for any given intensity. In fact, heart rates for erging and rowing are not the same. Some research indicates that heart rates on the water can be as much as 10 beats higher than on an ergometer for the same oxygen consumption. There is also evidence that rowers who train on water year round have 'on-water' heart rates lower than on the ergometer. This brings us to **rule one of heart rate monitoring. Heart rates are activity specific.**

Heart rate is influenced by many variables. Duration of training,

Figure 4. Determining Maximum Heart Rate

A progressive incremental test is like a stair case. Each step is 3 minutes long. At the end of each step the heart rate is recorded and the intensity is increased by a predetermined increment. When the subject cannot go any farther or the intensity is increased but the heart rate does not go up the test is stopped. The highest heart rate achieved during the test is the maximum heart rate.

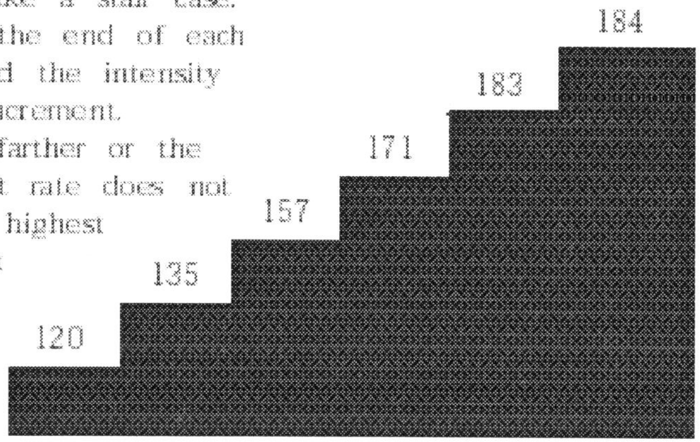

emotional stress, clothing, heat, dehydration, overtraining, loss of sleep, decreased blood volume, altitude, and detraining all change the heart-rate response. During long duration steady-state training sessions (60 minutes or more) the heat produced by the body has been shown to increase heart rate by as much as 20 beats per minute. If you were to slow down to try to keep your heart rate the same, you would change the training effect for the muscles. This leads us to heart-rate **rule two: During steady-state training the boat speed or power output should remain constant throughout the session regardless of increases in heart rate.**

Training in a hot environment can increase heart rate by up to 13 beats per minute. This can make the accurate use of heart rate very difficult. Late in a training cycle heart rates can be different than what they were a week earlier for the same power output. Whether this is higher or lower is difficult to predict. Emotional stress at work or the stress of exams at schools tends to increase heart rate during training. In addition, these types of stress decrease quality of sleep which further increases heart rate. **Rule three: When training in hot weather or during periods of high stress use feelings of fatigue and comfort as a training guide rather than heart rate.**

Heart rate is an individual response as is maximum heart rate. For example, people in the same boat may have 20 to 30 beat differences in heart rates during the same training session. This isn't necessarily due to differences in fitness rather it is something inherent to those people. Comparing heart rates with others is unnecessary and often unwise. Training programs should not be based on general heart-rate guidelines, but should be based on individual responses. A training heart rate of 150 bpm may elicit very different adaptations for different people. **Rule four: Don't compare heart rates with others.**

Because heart rate is an individual response and because it can be dependent on fitness level. Heart rate values need to be determined in relation to other physiological variables. There are three common physiological markers for aerobic training: Aerobic threshold, anaerobic threshold and VO2 max. Training programs are normally designed with the idea of changing these physiological points. In order to prescribe meaningful heart rate ranges these points have to be identified. This can be done through lactate testing or through an oxygen consumption test. The data is then plotted and meaningful heart rate ranges can be developed. If these points are not determined the heart rate prescriptions are purely guess work. **Rule five: Heart rate ranges should be determined from other physiological data.**

As mentioned earlier, heart rate is not a good tool for monitoring intensity during speed work or interval training. Some coaches believe heart rate should be used to monitor recovery between intervals so fatigue levels can be controlled. While it is true that fatigue levels need to be controlled, heart rate is not the way to do it. The fatigue during high-intensity rowing is caused primarily by lactic acid accumulation. The time between intervals should be based on the time needed to reduce lactate levels. The relationship between heart rate recovery and lactate recovery is not very strong. In other words, heart rate may have recovered but the lactate levels may still be too high to do the interval the way it should be done.

Heart rate is a tool for training. Like all tools it has limitations and should be used for a specific job at a specific time. Boat speed or power output on the ergometer are influenced by fewer factors than heart rate, and may prove to be better indicators of training intensity. If you are going to use heart rate to monitor your intensity follow the guidelines outlined here and remember that heart rate is just a response to internal and external stimuli, it should not be the main controlling factor for your training.

Field/Performance Testing

Using a performance or field test to predict the training categories relies on the relationship between the time to fatigue and aerobic or anaerobic threshold.

Anaerobic threshold has been shown to be an intensity that can be held for 20 to 30 minutes. A 20-minute performance test can be used to estimate the training categories. In the 20-minute test, the athlete is required to row as many meters as possible in 20 minutes. Dr. Volker Nolte, Canadian lightweight men's coach and a professor at University of Western Ontario, has developed some guidelines for using a 20-minute test to predict categories (table 6).

Estimates from a performance test to categories can be affected by several factors. Performance tests do not rely only on the physiological capacity of the athlete. A good score on a performance test is a function of physiological, mental, technical, and tactical components working together. There are many athletes who either under or over perform according to their physiological data simply because they did not treat the test like a race and were not properly prepared mentally.

The guidelines in Table 6 are most accurate near anaerobic threshold. The majority of the data used to develop these guidelines used National team calibre athletes. They tend to overestimate category VI in lower level athletes. This is probably because national level athletes have spent more training time in category VI and understand how a category VI session feels. Most lower level athletes, when attempting a category VI session, are actually in category V because they have never accurately had categories determined. This leads to fitness increases in category V without much change in category VI causing this category to be lower than expected.

Table 6. Prediction of Training Categories from a Performance Test

Using the average 500 m splits from a 20 minute test

Category III is 2 seconds faster
Category IV is 2 seconds slower
Category V is 8 seconds slower
Category VI is 13 seconds slower

Example: If the athlete rows 6000 m in 20 minutes the average split/500m would be 1:40 therefore:

Category III is   1:38
Category IV is   1:42
Category V is   1:48
Category VI is   1:53

This method is much more accurate than predicting heart rate ranges because the performance test individualises the result more than heart rate estimates. Since this test does not rely on a heart rate deflection point it is easier to perform and possibly more accurate than the Conconi test.

Conclusion

Coaches put hours into developing training programs with the hope that athletes will adapt and achieve their best performance. Athletes spend and equal or greater amount of time executing the program that they believe is going to help them achieve their goals.

Determining training categories through direct measures is relatively inexpensive ($50 to $150) and can help ensure that the hours of training are as efficient and effective as possible. In the event that facilities for the direct measure of training categories are not available, a 20-minute performance test can provide a reasonable estimate of training categories.

References

Anulo, S. and Rusko, H. (1986). Aerobic and anaerobic thresholds determined from venous lactate or from ventilation and gas exchange in relation to muscle fibre composition. Int. J. Sports Med. (7):161-166.

Bourgois, J. and Vrijens, J (1998). The Conconi test: a controversial concept for the determination of anaerobic threshold in young rowers. Int. J. Sports Med. (19):553-559.

Caiozzo, V. et al. (1982). A comparison of gas exchange indices used to detect the anaerobic threshold. J. Appl. Physiol. (53): 1184-1189.

Conconi, F. et al (1996). The Conconi test: methodology after 12 years of application. Int. J. Sports Med. (17):509-519.

Conconi, F. et al. (1982). Determination of the anaerobic threshold by a noninvasive field test in runners. J. Appl. Physiol. (52) 869-873.

Davis, J. et al. (1976). Anaerobic threshold and maximal aerobic power for three modes of exercise. J. Appl. Physiol. (41): 544-550.

Droghetti, P. (1986). Determination of the anaerobic threshold on a rowing ergometer by the relationship between work output and heart rate. Scand J. Sci. (8): 59-62.

Hughes, E., Turner, S. and Brooks, G. (1982). effects of glycogen depletion and pedalling speed on anaerobic threshold. J. Appl. Physiol. (52): 1598-1607.

Poole, D., and Gasser, G. (1985). Response of ventilatory and lactate thresholds to continuous and interval training. J. Appl. Physiol. (58): 1115-1121.

Reinhard, U., Muller, P., and Schmulling, R. (1979). Determination of anaerobic threshold by ventilation equivalent in normal individuals. Respiration. (38): 36-42.

Simon, J. et al. (1983). Lactate accumulation relative to the anaerobic and respiratory compensation threshold. J. Appl. Physiol. (54):13-17.

Thoden, J.S. Aerobic Power in Physiological Testing of the High Performance Athlete. Human Kinetics Publishers. (1991)

Wasserman, K., and McIlroy, M. (1964). Detecting the threshold of anaerobic metabolism in cardiac patients during exercise. Am. J. Cardiol. (14) 844-852.

Introduction to Planning and Periodization

4

The annual physical training plan is a map that the athlete and coach use to guide them through the year. A good training plan has many characteristics that work together to bring the athlete or team to peak form.

Characteristics of a Training Plan

Flexibility

The training plan is not the law. It is a guideline set out at the beginning of the year. It should be flexible because the exact response of an individual to a training session cannot be predicted months in advance. If the training plan is made for a team, it should be flexible enough to take into account the individual needs and schedules of the athletes involved. A flexible training plan will have a greater level of compliance than one that doesn't take into account individual differences and unpredictable events.

However, there is a limit to the flexibility of a training plan. If the plan is too flexible it will give the impression of lack of organization. A poorly organized plan will not allow the athletes to reach their goals and makes goal setting difficult.

Goal Oriented

Goal setting is the cornerstone of the training plan. Without goals the training plan and athlete have no specific direction. Designing a training plan without goals is like building a house without a blueprint – it isn't impossible but it is very difficult.

The Benefits of Goal Setting

Both the coach and athlete should participate in the goal setting process. There are several reasons for establishing goals for the upcoming season:

- Direction is established and priorities are set
- Concrete goals increase motivational levels in both the coach and athlete
- Provide a basis for measurable success
- Improves communication between athlete and coach
- Helps develop psychological maturity
- Prevention of problem behavior
- Develops an appreciation of planning and goal setting
- Happier athletes

Establishing Goals

Goals have to be realistic and attainable. There are two types of goals that must be set – short-term and long-term goals. Long-term goals represent the ultimate end point for the athlete, i.e. competing in the Olympics or winning the World Championships, or the point he or she wants to reach at the end of a training year. Each year, the athlete should develop such a goal. Short-term goals are then used as steps to help them get to the long-term goal. Short-term goals should be attainable in a reasonable period of time (several weeks). The following process can be used to establish long-term and short-term goals:

- Develop a set of goals that you feel are reasonable for the upcoming year
- Ask the athlete to develop a similar set of goals
- Meet with the athlete, discuss the two sets of goals and come to

an agreement as to the goals for the upcoming season (make sure this is a discussion and that you are not dictating goals to the athlete).
- When goals have been decided upon make them very clear. Write them down and attach time lines to each goal.

Do not be afraid to adjust the short-term goals as the year progresses. If a goal is not reached in the estimated time, it does not mean the athlete has failed it only means that the time for reaching the goal was underestimated.

Following up on the Goals

Once goals have been established there has to be a follow up process. The goals should be periodically reviewed to ensure that they are still relevant and realistic. Behavior that is consistent with the goals should be encouraged.

Parents, if the athlete is under the age of majority, should be informed about the goals that have been set. Since parents form a large part of the support network for many athletes, they can have a strong impact on whether the goal is achieved or not.

Periodic Check Ups

Some method of monitoring the effectiveness of the training plan should be built into the plan. Periodic check ups help to ensure the set goals can be reached. They give the coach some concrete data upon which to base changes in the training plan. These check ups can take on a variety of forms. Monitoring of training log books, fitness assessments, evaluation of performances, or interviews with the athlete are all valuable ways of checking progress.

Periodized

The training plan must be periodized. It is impossible to train all the necessary components of a sport at one time there should be periods during the year where certain things are emphasized while others are maintained. All elements of an athlete's preparation should be periodized including physical preparation, psychological preparation and skill development. Periodization is usually done by following the logical break up of the competitive year into training phases.

Training Phases

The year can be broken up into logical training periods such as the preparatory phase, the competitive phase, and the transition phase (Bompa, 1983).

The Preparatory Phase

The preparatory phase falls at the beginning of the training year. The preparatory phase can be further divided into general preparation and specific preparation periods. The general preparation is the first and longest of the preparation phases. Generally, 12 to 24 weeks are required for this phase. The goal of the general preparation phase is to improve on areas of weakness and to build a base for higher intensity specific preparation. Rehabilitation of injuries or muscle imbalances created during the previous season are corrected during the first part of this phase. During this phase general strength training, flexibility and aerobic conditioning are emphasized. A long, productive general preparation phase will allow the athlete to reach a high peak for a major competition.

In rowing, the training volumes tend to be slightly lower during the general prep phase. Almost all aerobic training will be done in category VI with possibly one each of categories V and IV. Because of the emphasis on category VI cross training can be used during the general prep phase to eleviate boredom and help prevent overuse injuries. The specific preparation phase is eight to 16 weeks long and takes advantage of the base developed during the general preparation phase. The newly acquired fitness is put to work in sport specific situations. There is more emphasis placed upon specific aerobic, anaerobic and power work in this phase. Training volumes increase through the specific prep phase. By the end of the phase, the training sessions should very closely imitate competitive situations as far as movement patterns, speed, and work/rest intervals are concerned. There should be maintenance training sessions for strength and general aerobic conditioning built into this phase.

The preparation phases are the ideal time to emphasize skill development. Since the work volumes are high but the intensity of the activities is very low the athlete should not be experiencing high levels of fatigue that will negatively impact upon skill development or perfection (Bompa, 1983). The general prep phase is an excellent time to work on individual parts of a skill that may need perfecting (i.e. body position during the leg drive feathering the blade, etc.). The specific prep phase should see the beginnings of combining the parts of the skills into the whole skill.

The Pre-Competitive Phase

The pre-competitive phase, or pre-season, normally lasts four to eight weeks. There is a greater emphasis on the development of on water speed during this phase. Categories IV, III, and II become more important. Often crew selection takes place during this time.

The Competitive Phase

This is the phase where all the important competitions occur. In cases where the competitive season is very long it can be broken into early and late-competitive phases. The early competitive phase becomes an extension of the pre-competitive phase in that there is a greater emphasis placed on physical preparation. The main competition for the year will normally fall at the end of the late competitive phase.

During this phase the emphasis is on technical work. The physical preparation is limited to maintenance work and pre-competition peaking cycles. All the training sessions should be sport specific. Where possible there should be a combination of skill development and tactical development at the same time. This means that a certain level of ingenuity is necessary on the part of the coach and athlete in order to develop drills that will accomplish both objectives. This is the first phase that is placed into the training plan and the lengths of all the other phases are dependent upon this one. The development of physical preparation is usually of secondary importance during this phase. Training should be done to maintain the fitness level developed during the preparatory and pre competitive phases.

Perfection of skill and development of competitive experience are the primary emphasis during this phase. Skill development should emphasize the perfection of the complete rowing stroke. The fine tuning of specific parts of the rower's technique are crucial during this phase.

The Transition Phase

This phase follows the competitive phase. This is a period of several weeks where the athlete has a break from training. Athletes should be encouraged to keep active during this period by doing activities not related to their sport. This phase allows time for physical and mental recovery after a hard training and competitive schedule. Typically, this phase will last for two to four weeks.

Training Cycles

The training phases represent the gross structures of a training plan. Each training phase should be broken down into smaller segments known as training cycles, it is through these training cycles that the volume and intensity of work are controlled.

Training cycles are smaller sub-divisions of the training phase. There are two types of training cycles that we will discuss, the macrocycle and the microcycle. Macrocycles can vary in length from two to six weeks but are typically about four weeks long. Microcycles are the usually about a week long and represent possibly the most important training plan division (Bompa, 1983).

Macrocycles

Length of a macrocycle

The length of a macrocycle can vary from two to six weeks in duration. The length of a macrocycle can be determined in several ways;

- the time it takes to learn a part of a skill,
- the time it takes to develop a physical quality,
- the time it takes to master a tactical component

can all be used as the criteria for setting the length of the macrocycle. The criteria that you decide to use will depend upon what qualities your athletes need to develop (physical, technical, mental, etc.).

During the preparation phases the length of the macrocycle is often set according to the time it takes to develop physical qualities (strength, endurance, power, etc.). During the pre-competitive phase you may want to use the time necessary for the development of a part of a skill as the basis for the macrocycle length. During the competitive season, the macrocycle length is dictated by the competition calendar which can vary from athlete to athlete depending on the competitions that are to be attended. Macrocycles should be planned so that they end near the day of an important competition or testing session. The results of the competition or test will allow the coach to establish the effectiveness of the macrocycle.

Goal Setting and Macrocycles

Each macrocycle should be constructed around definite reachable goals. The short term goals that were discussed earlier form the basis for the goals of the macrocycles. At the end of each macrocycle there should be a method for determining if the goals of that macrocycle were achieved.

Training log books are useful in determining if the goals were achieved. Log books can also be used to evaluate if the plan is being followed or not. Often, a coach will develop a great plan on paper and then for a variety of reasons not be able to follow it. This happens with young or inexperienced coaches. Log books allow the comparison of the intended and actual training programs. If they are extremely different then something should be done to try to make them similar. This may mean a revamping of the original training plan.

In addition to training logs regular performance and physiological tests should be conducted. Performance tests should be conducted at the end of the recovery week of each training cycle.

Designing a Macrocycle

A macrocycle is made up of microcycles (training weeks). Each microcycle will have a general intensity trend, i.e. high, medium or low intensity, that dictates how a macrocycle looks. In the next few pages you will find several macrocycle diagrams. Take some time to think about these and discuss them with other coaches.

Figure 1 shows a macrocycle that consists of three weeks where the intensity of activity is increasing each week. On the fourth week, the intensity decreases and the athlete is allowed to recover from the loading of the previous three weeks. The recovery week in all macro cycles is very important because much of the training improvement will be seen following recovery rather than during training.

Figure 2 shows a loading pattern that is often used during the early stages of the preparation phase. The cycle is longer because the intensity of training is lower. The volume is maintained for a couple of weeks before an increase. This allows the athlete coming off of a transition to adapt gradually to the new training year.

Figure 3 shows a macrocycle that is often seen during the final part of the competitive phase just prior to the major competition of the year. During this time the athletes are tapering and there is a drop in training volume from week to week.

As a coach, you must decide the type of macrocycle that will work best for your athletes. Work and school commitments on the part of the athletes don't always make it possible to follow a traditional plan used by full time rowers. It may be necessary to experiment with different types and combinations of macrocycles until one is found that works best for each group of athletes. There are some guidelines that you can follow when designing your own macrocycles.

- Progress from low intensity to high intensity
- As intensity goes up volume comes down
- Keep volume and intensity changes to less than 10% per week
- Recovery weeks need to be included every four to six weeks

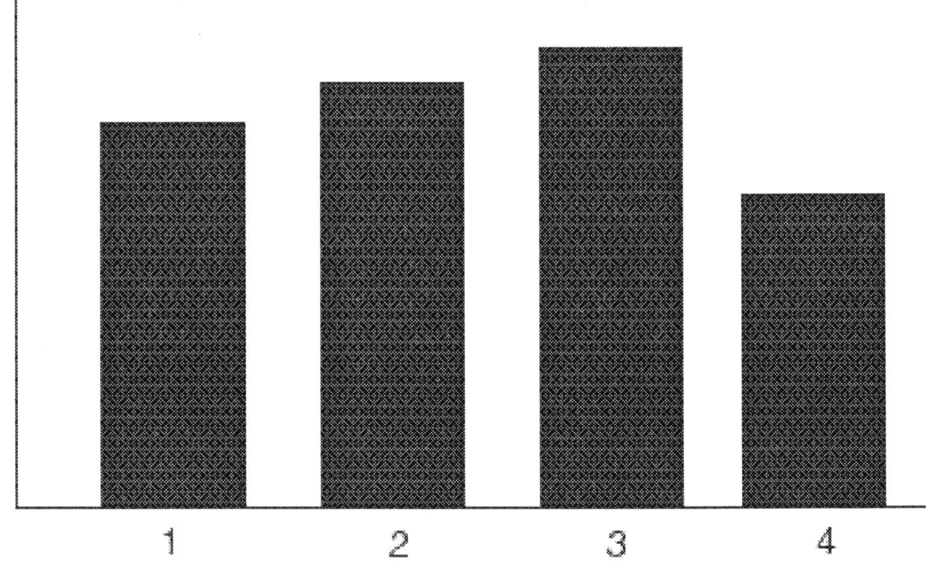

Figure 1. A typical macrocycle where 3 weeks of increasing volume are followed by a recovery week. During the recovery week the volume is reduced by 25-40% of the peak volume of the cycle

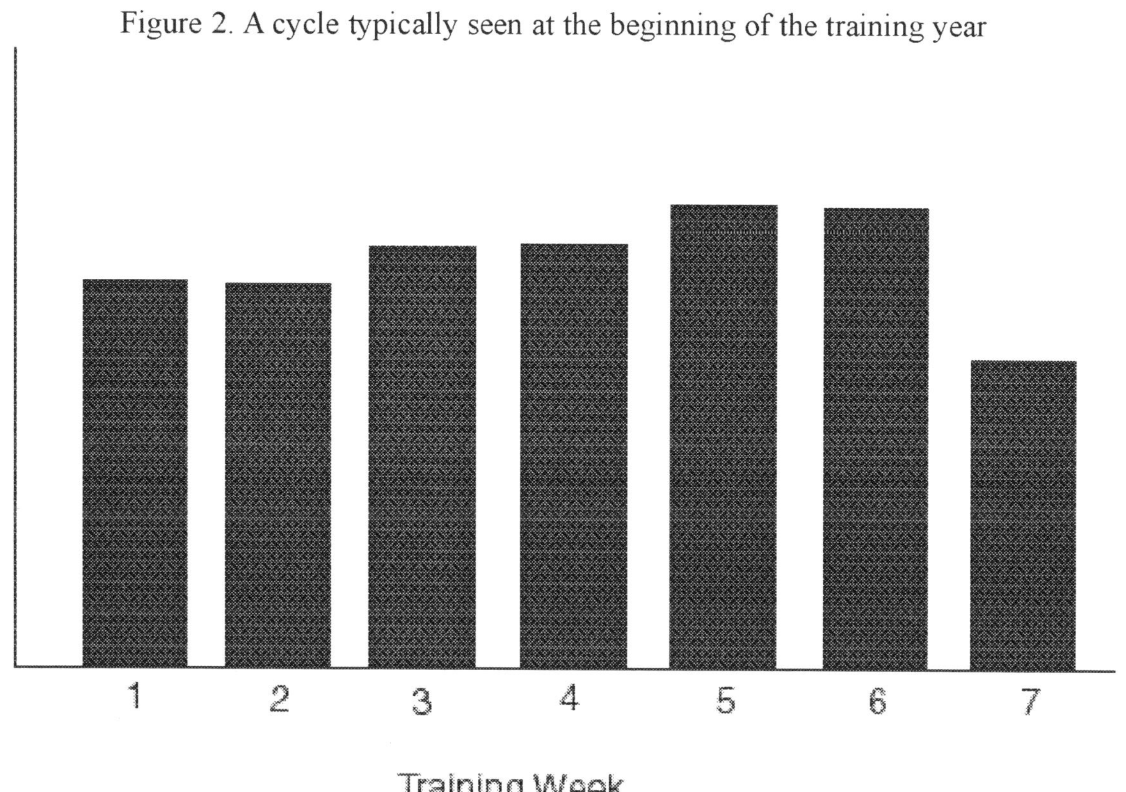

Figure 2. A cycle typically seen at the beginning of the training year
Training Volume (km)
Training Week
1
2
3
4
5
6
7

Figure 3. A cycle typically seen during the taper before a major competition. Volume drops by 50% between the first and third weeks

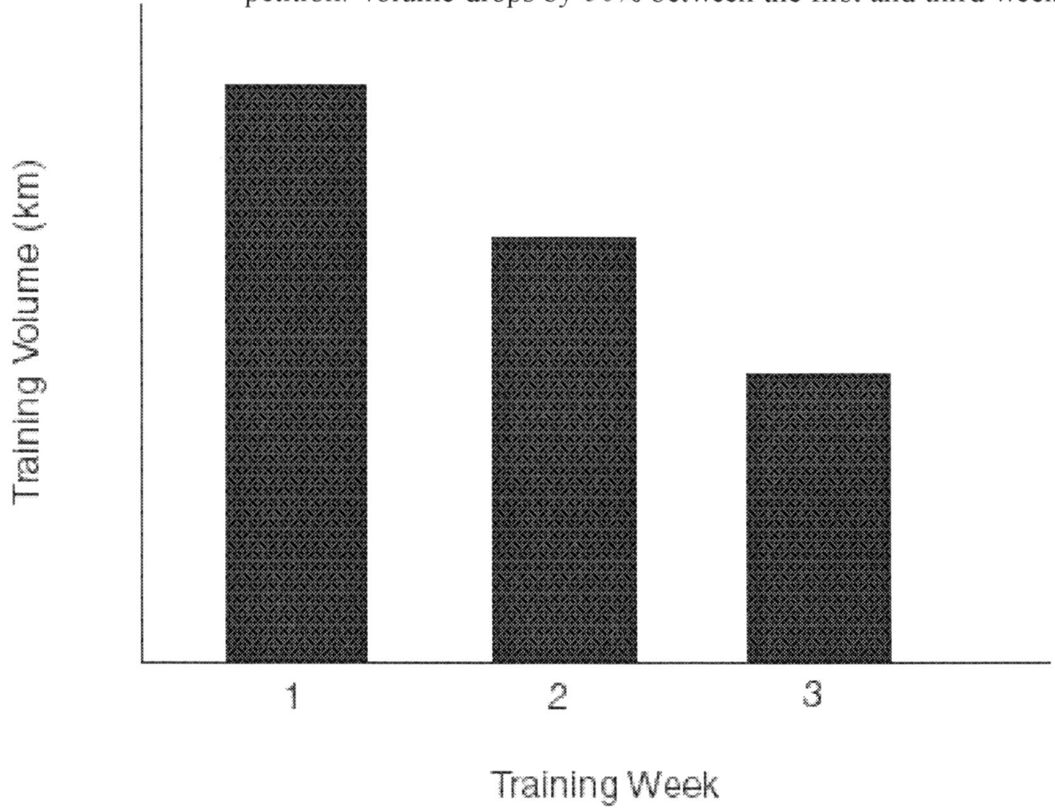

Designing a Microcycle

Microcycles are the most important part of the training plan. If the microcycles are not designed properly it does not matter how well the rest of the year is planned. Microcycles represent the weekly and daily variations in the training program.

One of the objectives of a microcycle is to distribute the training fatigue over the week to allow the athlete to accomplish as much work as possible while still having adequate recovery. There are four ways that this is commonly accomplished.

Front loaded

In a front-loaded week, the first three to four days of the week have the highest training volumes. There is a continuous drop in volume through the week. This allows the athlete to complete the most work while their energy stores are full from a day off and lower training volumes later in the week. This type of cycle can be useful for athletes who go to school or work full time. The training week can run from Friday to Friday leaving the weekend available for higher volumes of training. The seventh day of the week is off. This is typical of all microcycles, at least one day per week is set aside as a complete rest day. The coach should recommend the athlete not participate in physically demanding recreational activities on the rest day. Failure to take a complete day of rest may make it more difficult to do the planned volume and intensity during the next week.

End loaded

An end-loaded week is the opposite of a front-loaded week. The training volume is gradually increased throughout the week. Since the biggest training day is the last day of the week the athlete must pay closer attention to what they eat during the week. One advan-

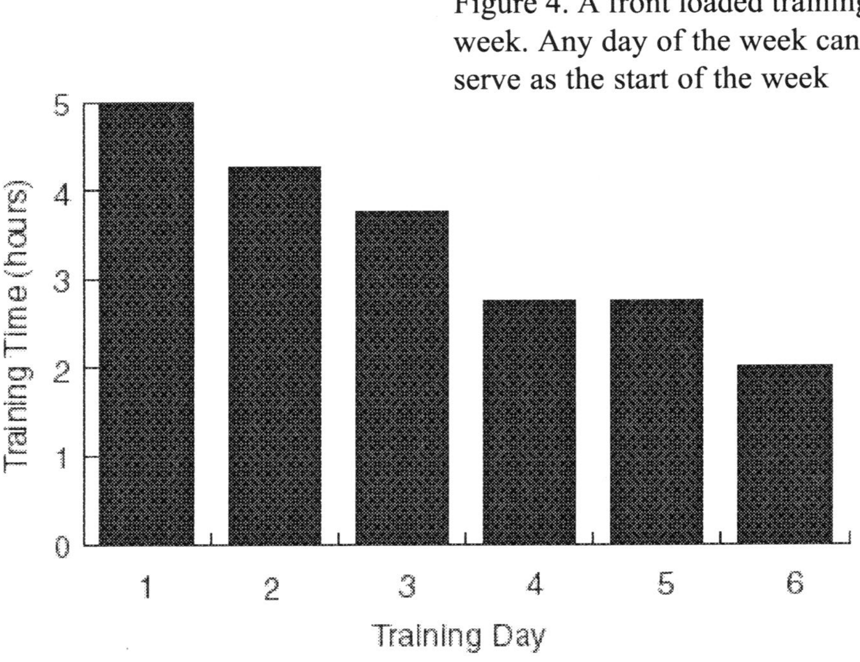

Figure 4. A front loaded training week. Any day of the week can serve as the start of the week

tage of this type of microcycle is athletes may be more inclined to push themselves on the highest volume day, because of the time off the following day.

Alternate load

In an alternate load week high- and low-volume days are alternated. This method is used to ensure adequate recovery between training sessions. This type of microcycle is most effective with beginning and master level rowers whose recovery ability is less than that of elite performers. This type of microcycle may also be beneficial to lightweight rowers who are trying to make weight. Periods of food restriction will increase the time needed to recover between higher

100

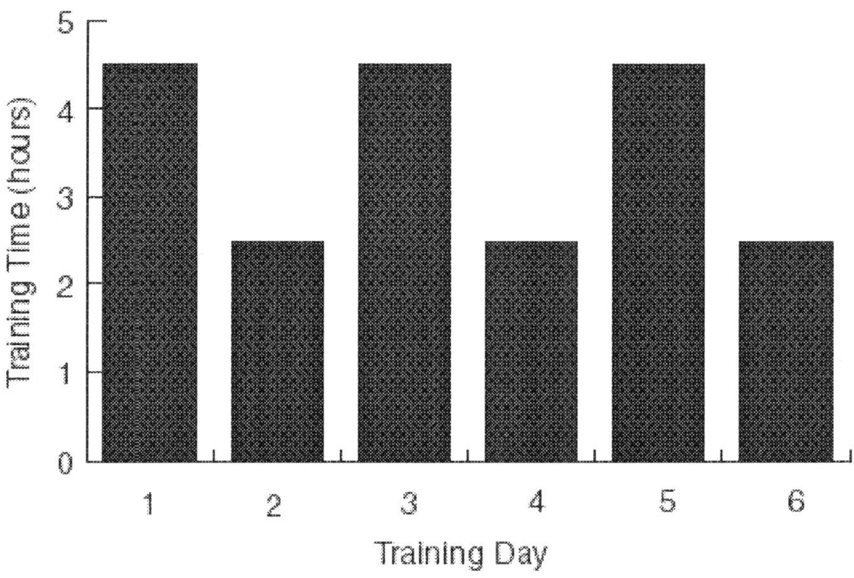

volume training days.

Even load distribution

Even load distribution is as the name applies. The weeks training volume is divided evenly over the six training days. Fatigue accumulates slowly throughout the week. The main disadvantage to this system is that athletes are tempted to pace themselves early in the week so that they can get through all the sessions. The end of the week is psychologically difficult if the intensity was too high earlier in the week.

Figure 6. Even-load distribution

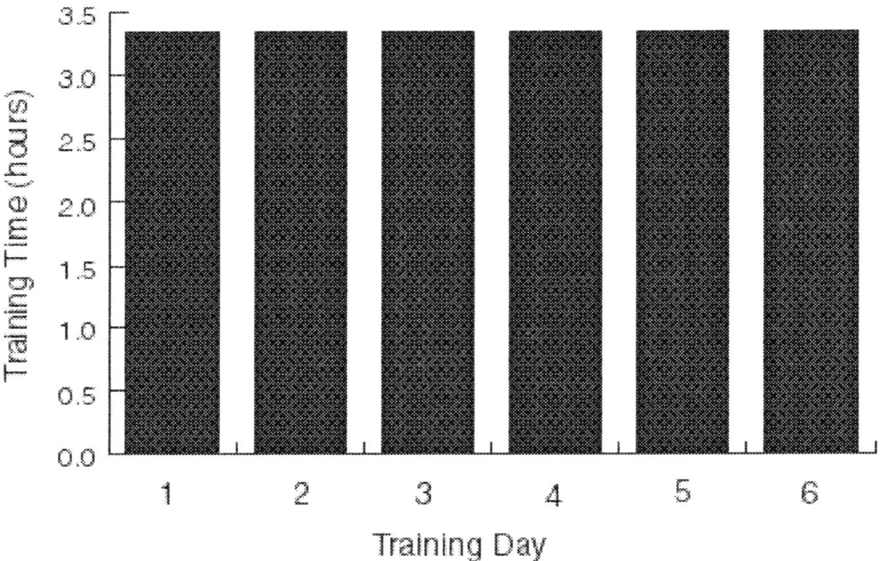

Pyramidal loading

When using a pyramidal loading scheme the training volume peaks at mid-week. This type of loading is particularly useful during the first week of a macrocycle following a recovery week. The athlete is allowed to gradually get back into full training in the first two days of the week. Psychologically, it allows the athlete to push themselves on each session knowing that the volume gradually decreases towards the end of the week.

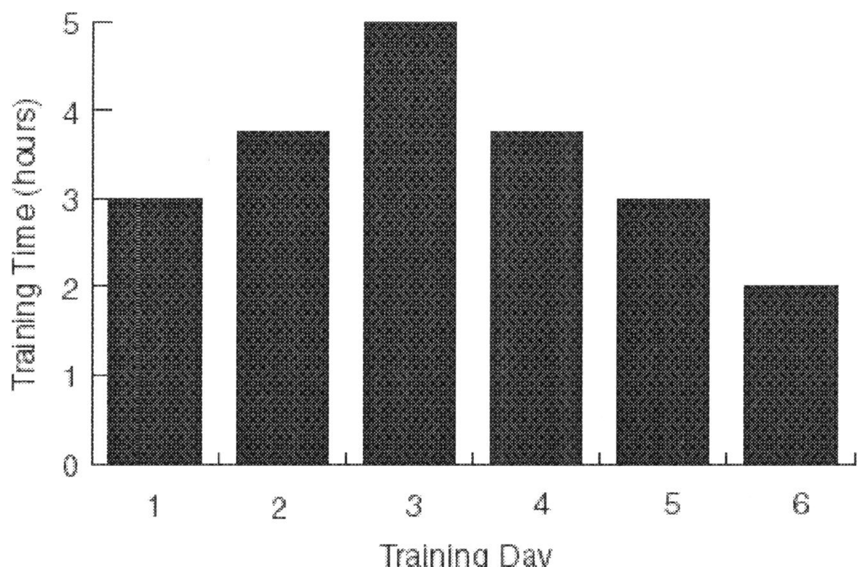

Conclusion

Training cycles are an important part of the training plan. When properly developed, they ensure the athlete is working toward goals. Training cycles are also instrumental in the prevention of overtraining.

It may take some time and practice to become comfortable designing training cycles. Keep practicing and be patient, make sure records are kept of how athletes react to different types of training cycles. Learning how each athlete responds to training or competition and then adapting the program to suit their needs is part of the art of coaching.

References

Bompa, T. (1983). Theory and Methodology of Training: The key to Athletic Performance. Dubuque, Iowa: Kendall/Hunt Publishing Company.

Coaching Association of Canada National Coaching Certification Program Level 2 Course Conductor Manual.

Periodized Model of Strength Training for Rowing

5

Race rowing consists of an all-out effort for six to seven minutes. During this time the aerobic, anaerobic alactic, and anaerobic lactic systems are maximally stressed (Steinacker, 1993). Muscular strength also plays an important role in race performance. Although the benefits of strength training for rowing have been questioned (Secher, 1993), most rowers participate in some form of strength and power training during the off season (Hagerman and Staron, 1983).

Strength training for rowing has traditionally consisted of either resistance training or circuit weight training (Hagerman and Staron, 1983). Many coaches and athletes are unsure about the most effective and efficient way of designing their strength programs. The purpose of this chapter is to present the physiological basis of strength training for rowing and a model from which strength training programs can be developed.

Strength Demands of Rowing

Since the validity of strength training has been questioned (Secher, 1993) it is important that the strength demands of rowing are established. Ishiko (1967) used strain gauge dynamometers mounted on

Table 1. Force Production During Rowing

Phase	Time Interval	Stroke Rate (strokes/min)	Peak Force (N)
Start Spurt	0-10s	36-42	1000-1500
Start Phase	10-60s	34-38	600-800
Race	1-5 min	30-36	500-700
Final Spurt	5-6 min	34-38	600-700

the oars to measure the forces generated by the silver medal winning eights from the Tokyo Olympics. It was found that the forces ranged from 70 to 90 kg. A specially instrumented Gjessing ergometer has been used by Hartmann, Mader, Wasser and Klauer (1993) to investigate the forces developed during the first five strokes of a six-minute maximal test. They tested 81 members of the German national squads and found that in the men, the highest forces were obtained in the first stroke and were on the order of 1352 N. For the women, the highest forces were also during the first stroke and averaged 1019 N. Secher (1975), using the winning time from the eights in the 1972 World Championships, has calculated that a minimum rowing strength of 133 kg is essential for international competition. Steinacker (1993) presented a compilation of data obtained in the former East Germany. This can be seen in Table 1.

The data in Table 1 indicate that rowers require a high level of maximal strength and strength endurance.

Strength Levels of Rowers

Many different protocols, ranging from traditional methods to sport specific methods, have been used to evaluate the strength of rowers. In order to study maximal force generation at the catch Secher (1975) developed an isometric apparatus that was adjustable so as to suit individual rowing positions. Using Dutch Olympic, national, and club level rowers it was found that international rowers on average generated 204 kg of force. National level rowers generated 183 kg of force and club rowers generated 162 kg of force. Using other non-specific rowing tests – isometric arm pull, back extension, trunk flexion and leg extension – on the same groups of athletes, Secher (1975) found that the higher the competition level of the rower the greater the strength in all tests. The strength levels of some international calibre rowers are comparable to those of high-level power-lifters or body builders (Larsson and Forsberg, 1980). Strength levels of rowers are most pronounced at low velocities (Larsson and Forsberg, 1980; Hagerman and Staron, 1984). This may be due to the large percentage of slow twitch fibres found in competitive rowers.

Muscle Fibre Type and Rowing

Muscle fibres, in humans, can be divided into two broad categories – a summary of the fibre types can be seen in Table 2. Slow twitch (ST), also known as type I fibres, are capable of working for extended periods of time. This is due, in part, to their metabolic profile which favours energy production through aerobic pathways (Salmons, 1994). Fast twitch fibres can be subdivided into three categories. Fast twitch glycolytic (FT), type IIb, fibres produce energy predominantly through anaerobic pathways and are capable of high power production, but only for short periods of time (Salmons, 1994). Fast twitch oxidative-glycolytic (FOG), type IIa, are not as adept at power production as the FT fibres, but they produce more power than the ST fibres. The FOG fibres are capable of generating energy through both aerobic and anaerobic pathways, this makes them an endurance fibre of intermediate power production

Figure 1. Relative Fibre Areas for Rowers

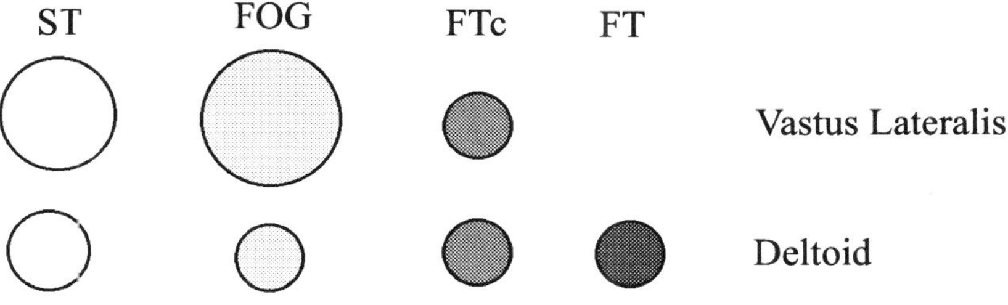

(Salomons, 1994). The final type of fast twitch fibre is the undifferentiated fast twitch (FTc) or type IIc fibre. The functions and metabolic capacities of this fibre are, at present, not completely understood. It is however, thought that these fibres are in the process of becoming either FOG or FT fibres (Larsson and Forsberg, 1980).

Rowers, like other endurance athletes, tend to have a high percentage of ST fibres. This may seem surprising since individuals with large muscle mass tend to have higher percentages of FT fibres (Larsson and Forsberg, 1980). Muscle fibre type studies have shown that oarsmen have 70 to 85% ST fibres (Roth, Schwanitz, Pas, and Bauer, 1993; Larsson and Forsberg, 1980; Hagerman and Staron, 1983; Steinacker, 1993). Oarswomen also have large percentages of ST fibres, about 65%, but not as high as the men (Clarkson, Graves, and Melchionda, 1984). In contrast 40 to 50% of the muscle fibres from normal, sedentary people are slow twitch (Larsson, Grimby and Karlsson, 1979). Not only do rowers have a large percentage of ST fibres by number but these fibres are also hypertrophied. There is no significant difference between the cross sectional area between fast and slow twitch fibres (Roth, Schwanitz, Pas, and Bauer, 1993; Larsson and Forsberg, 1980; Hagerman and Staron, 1983; Steinacker, 1993).

It is interesting to note that only four to 9% of the fibres are of the FT type (Roth, Schwanitz, Pas, and Bauer, 1993; Larsson and Forsberg, 1980; Hagerman and Staron, 1983; Steinacker, 1993; Clarkson, Graves, and Melchionda, 1984) in both men and women. Essentially, the skeletal muscle of rowers are composed largely of slow twitch and fast oxidative glycolytic muscle. This fibre type distribution can have a profound influence on the development of training programs, and particularly strength training programs.

The Strength Training Program

Strength training, as with aerobic, anaerobic, and skill training, should be periodized (Stone and O' Bryant, 1987). The program presented here is divided into General Preparation, Specific Preparation, Pre-Competitive, and Competitive phases.

General Preparation Phase

The General Preparation phase, consists of two training cycles and lasts for a maximum of 15 weeks. The first cycle is designed for the teaching of exercise technique, preparation for higher intensity work and the re-establishment of bilateral symmetry. Kramer, Leger, and Morrow (1991) have found that sweep rowing results in strength differences between oarside and nonoarside leg strength. Whether there is a technical advantage or disadvantage to this asymmetry is unclear. However, strength imbalances have been implicated in the development of injuries. This is normally corrected by using some unilateral exercises during the first three weeks of this phase. The last two weeks of the phase feature bilateral exercises where an emphasis is placed on lifting evenly. The second cycle of this phase focuses on developing a strength base and maximal strength.

General Preparation Phase: Cycle I: (3 to 5 weeks)

Purpose:

1.   Re-establish symmetry
2.   Teach exercise technique
3.   Prepare for high intensity training

Intensity: 50-70% 1RM

Volume: 30-40 per exercise

Sets: 3-5
Repetitions: 8-12
Exercises/Session: 3-5
Sessions/week: 3-6

Speed: Rate of 20-25 repetitions per minute

General Preparation Phase: Cycle II: (8-10 weeks)

Purpose:

1.   Development of Strength Base
2.   Development of Maximal Strength
3.   Prepare for power development

Intensity: 80-95 % 1RM

Volume: 8-25 reps per exercise

Sets: 3-5
Repetitions: 2-8
Exercises/session: 3-5
Sessions/week: 4-6

Speed: Rate of 20-30 repetitions per minute

The intensity of exercise during the general preparation phase varies from 50 to 95% of 1RM. The intensity is increased progressively throughout the phase and features two to three weeks of loading followed by lower intensity recovery phases (Bompa, 1983; Stone and

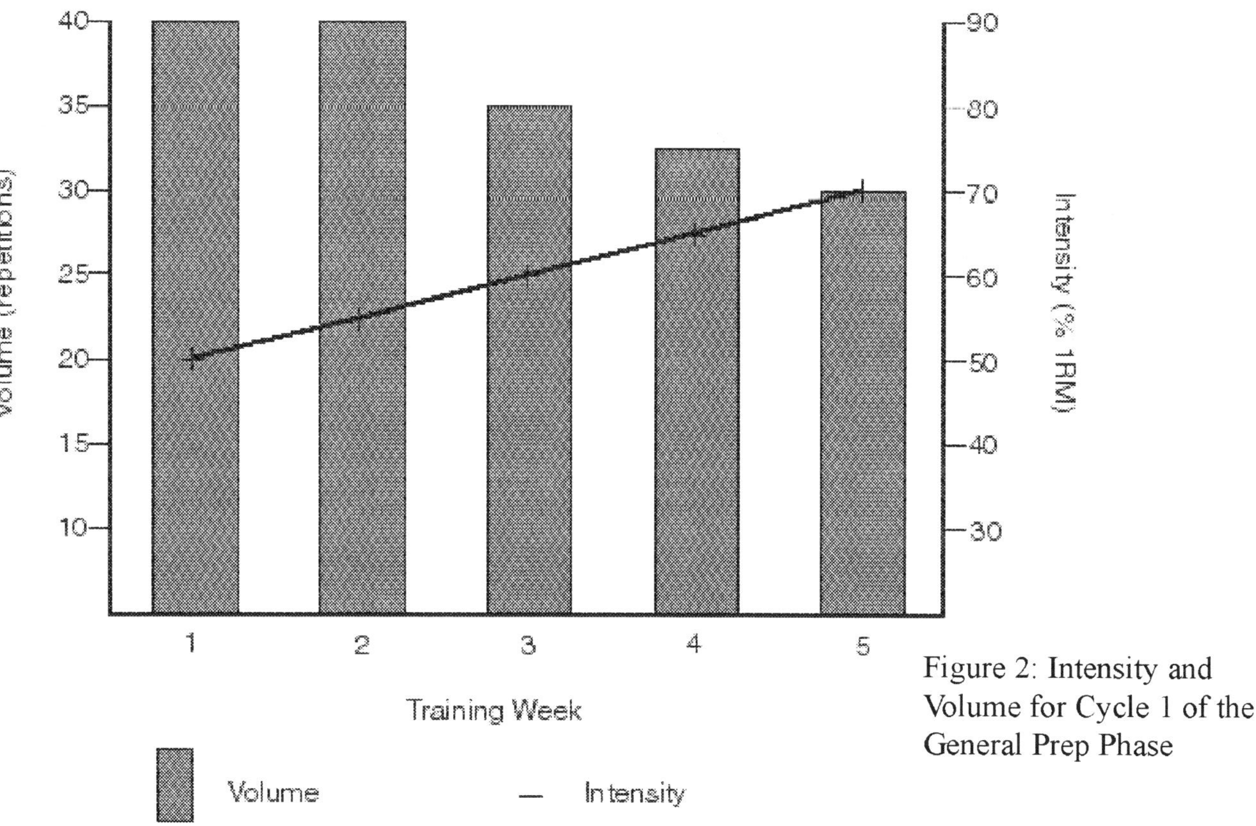

Figure 2: Intensity and Volume for Cycle 1 of the General Prep Phase

113

O'Bryant, 1987). The very low intensities during the initial weeks of this phase are designed to help the athlete learn proper exercise technique. Schmidt (1991) found that variability in movement pattern increases as the intensity of exercise increases and that skill learning is made more difficult as the variability in movement pattern increases. The second cycle of this phase features higher intensities and is characterized by periods of work that emphasizes muscular development, 70 to 80% 1RM, followed by periods that emphasize neuromuscular adaptations, 85 to 95% 1RM (Schmidtbleicher, 1985).

The volume of work decreases as the intensity increases. The athletes do not perform to muscular failure rather, they perform to technical failure. This has been found to help in the control of lactic acid levels (Reed, Ablack, McNeely, 1992) and helps improve total work volume per training session by allowing more sets to be performed with a given resistance. Technical failure has been defined as the point at which compensation movements occur, or help is needed to finish a repetition (Reed, Ablack, McNeely, 1992).

The speed of movement is one of the most important, and most neglected, variables in designing strength programs for rowing. In order to optimize improvements in power performance both the force and velocity components must be trained (Newton and Kraemer, 1994). As mentioned, rowers develop most of their force and power at relatively low velocities (Steinacker, 1993).   It has been found that strength adaptations are specific to the training speed (Behm and Sale, 1993; Sale and MacDougall 1981). In other words, training at high velocity increases strength at high velocity and training at low velocity increases strength at low velocity (Secher, 1993). This is due in part to neural adaptations (Knapik and Ramos, 1980), because high and low velocity movements require different neural recruitment and coordination. Training at lower velocity can allow the slow twitch fibres to contribute to the work (Faulkner, Claflin, and McCully, 1986). Since rowers possess such

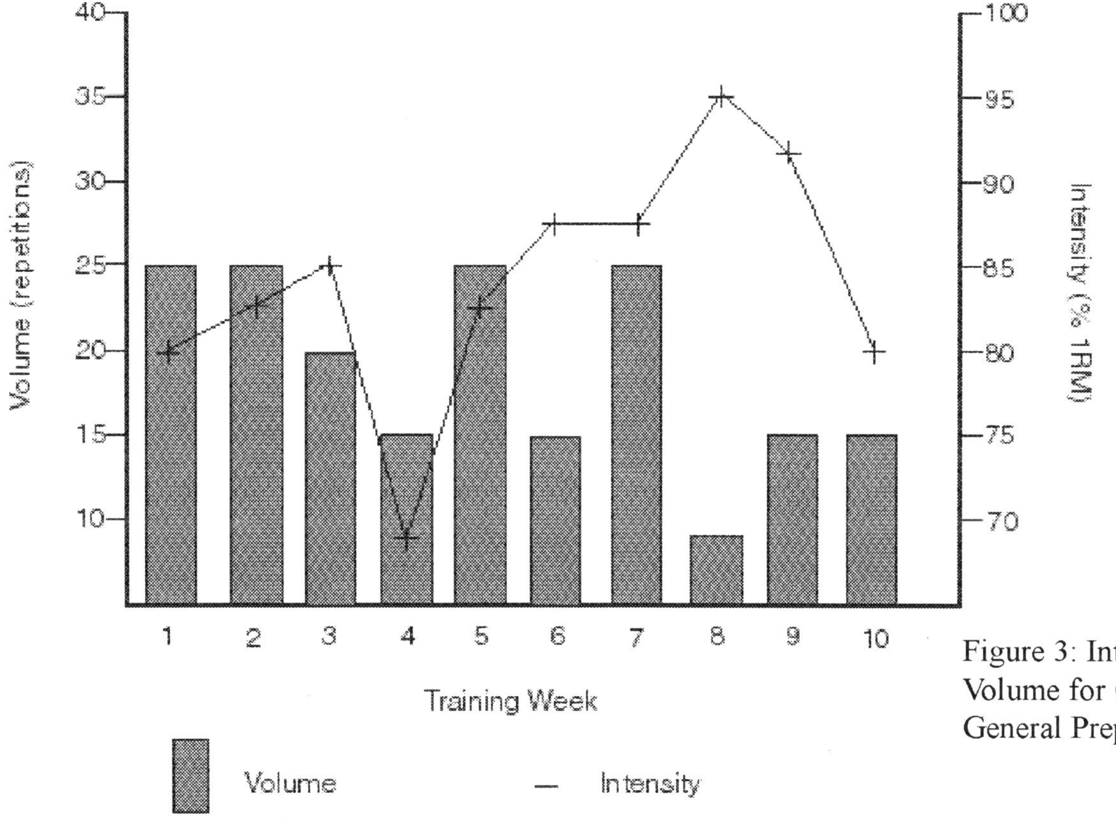

Figure 3: Intensity and Volume for Cycle 2 of the General Prep Phase

115

large percentages of slow twitch fibres it is imperative that they are trained for maximal force production. For this reason the training velocity during the general preparation phase is kept low.

During the second cycle of the general preparation phase there are two unloading weeks in which both the volume and intensity are dropped. Since there is an accumulation of fatigue from week to week this allows the athlete a rest week in which recovery and adaptation can occur.

Specific Preparation Phase

The specific preparation phase lasts for six to eight weeks and is designed to develop of rowing-specific power. Rowers experience a variety of power outputs throughout a race (Steinacker, 1993). For this reason, exercise intensity is periodized so that in the early weeks of this phase the rower becomes accustomed to developing power at high loads, as would be experienced during the start spurt. The final four weeks of the phase are designed for power endurance training. The intensities decrease to percentages of 1RM that would be similar to those experienced during a race (Hartmann, Mader, Wasser, and Klauer, 1993; Steinacker, 1993).

The number of repetitions will vary inversely with the intensity. In the final week of the phase, the rower should be working with close to 100 repetitions per set. The repetition range becomes very high at this point, and carries into the pre-competitive phase, because strength or power endurance is best developed by combining the appropriate relative portions of strength with the time demands of the sport (Schmidtbleicher, 1985; Verhoshansky, 1986).

During this phase the speed of movement approaches or slightly exceeds the stroke rate seen during racing (Steinacker, 1993). Emphasis should be placed on creating explosiveness at the beginning of the range of motion. This may help in the development of power early in the stroke cycle. Again, this is done to keep the strength and power demands of training similar to those seen during racing.

For this phase of training either traditional or circuit training can be used. If circuit training is chosen, upper- and lower-body exercises should be alternated. This will help decrease the negative impact lactic acid accumulation can have on the workout (Reed, Ablack, McNeely, 1991).

Specific Preparation Phase: Cycle I: (6 to 8 weeks)

Purpose:
1.	Development of rowing specific power
2.	Maintenance of strength
3.	Prepare for on-water power development

Intensity:	30-85% 1RM
Volume:	30-200

Sets:	2-5
Repetitions:	6-100
Exercises/session:	3-5
Sessions/week:	3-5

Speed: Rate of 38 to 45 repetitions per minute

Pre-Competitive Phase

The pre-competitive phase lasts for four to eight weeks and is designed to allow strength and power, developed during the other phases, to be transferred to on water performance. This is accomplished through on-water rowing with increased resistance

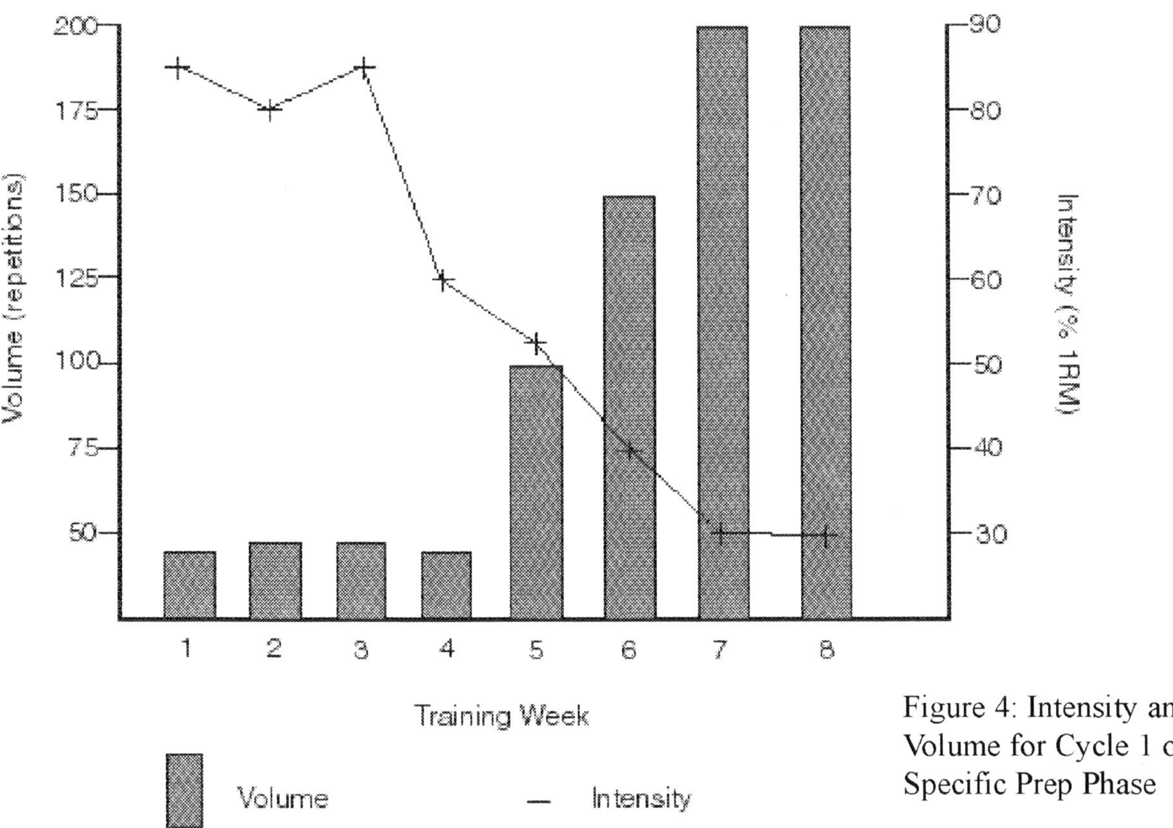

Figure 4: Intensity and Volume for Cycle 1 of the Specific Prep Phase

(Schmidtbleicher, 1985). This added resistance can take many forms i.e. dragging something behind the shell or having two people row in an eight. Since this type of strength work has to be very specific, technical performance should be watched very closely.

Intensity is varied by increasing or decreasing the amount of extra drag that is added. Rowers should be instructed to pull at full power for every stroke during this phase. It is very difficult to quantify intensity during this phase however, during training sessions boat speed can be used to determine decreases in intensity (assuming water conditions do not change).

There is a wide range of volumes in this phase. The selection of volume should be based upon training for specific phases of a race. Starts, finishes, and the rest of the race all have different strength, power and volume demands. The volume per set should be appropriately matched to the phase of the race that is being trained. Training with high volumes can be metabolically taxing on the athletes. Rest periods between sets should be relatively long, five to 10 minutes, and should involve very low intensity rowing. This should help in lactic acid removal and speed recovery between sets (McGrail, Bonen, and Belcastro, 1978).

Stroke rate should be close to race pace. However, it is probably unreasonable to assume that the athletes will be able to maintain maximal stroke rates with resistance added to the boat.

Pre-Competitive Phase: Cycle I: (4 to 8 weeks)

Purpose:
1.   Development of rowing specific power
2.   Transfer of power to on-water performance

Intensity: 30-50%

Full power rowing with resistance added to shell.

Volume: 50-250 strokes

Sets: 2-5
Repetitions: 10-120
Sessions/week: 2-3

Speed: Rate of 25-35 repetitions per minute

Notes:

Dry land strength maintenance should be done one to two times per week (see competitive phase for details).

Competitive Phase

The competitive phase lasts for the entire competitive season. The goal of strength training during this time is maintenance of strength developed during the off-season phases. This is extremely important for rowers since it has been found that rowers lose strength during the competitive season (Larsson and Forsberg, 1980).

Competitive Phase: Cycle I: (entire competitive season)

Purpose:

1.   Maintain strength that was built during the off season

Intensity: 70-80% 1RM
Volume: 20-40

Sets:	3-5
Repetitions:	6-12
Exercises/session:	3-5
Sessions/week:	1-2

Speed: Rate of 30 repetitions per minute

Strength maintenance can be accomplished through one to two dry-land sessions per week. Exercise intensity should be kept between 70% and 80% of 1RM. Exercise speed should be 25 to 30 repetitions per minute.

References

Behm, D.G., and Sale, D.G. (1993). Velocity specificity of resistance training. Sports Med. 15(6): 374-388.

Bompa, T. (1983). Theory and Methodology of Training: The key to Athletic Performance. Dubuque, Iowa: Kendall/Hunt Publishing Company.

Clarkson, P.M. , Graves, J., and Melchionda, A.m. (1984). Isokinetic strength and endurance and muscle fibre type of elite oarswomen. Can. J. Appl. Spt. Sci. 9(3): 127-132.

Faulkner, J.A., Claflin, D.R., and McCully, K.K. (1986). Power output of fast and slow fibres from human skeletal muscles. In Human Muscle Power. Jones, N.L., McCartney, N., and McComas, A.J. editors. Human Kinetics Publishers: Champaign, Ill.

Hagerman, F.C., and Staron, R.S. (1983). Seasonal variations among physiological variables in elite oarsmen. Can. J. Appl. Spt. Sci. 8(3):

143-148.

Hartman, U., Mader, A., Wasser, K., and Klauer, I. (1993). Peak force, velocity , and power during five and ten maximal rowing ergometer strokes by world class female and male rowers. Int. J. Sports Med. 14 (suppl1):S42-S45.

Ishiko, T. (1967). Application of telemetry to sport activities. Biomechanics. 1: 138-146.

Knapik, J., and Ramos, M. (1980). Isometric and isokinetic torque relationships in the human body. Arch. Phys. Med. Rehab. 61: 64-67.

Kramer, J.F., Leger, A., and Morrow, A. (1991). Oarside and nonoarside knee extensor strength measures and their relationship to rowing ergometer performance. JOSPT. 14(5): 213-219.

Larsson, L., and Forsberg, A. (1980). Morphological muscle characteristics in rowers. Can. J. Appl. Spt. Sci. 5(4): 239-244.

Larsson, L, Grimby, G., and Karlsson, (1979). Muscle strength and speed of movement in relation to age and muscle morphology. J. Appl. Physiol. 46(3): 451-456.

McGrail, J.C., Bonen, A., and Belcastro, A.N. (1978) Dependence of Lactate Removal on Muscle Metabolism in Man. Eur. J Appl. Physiol. 39: 89-97.

Newton, R.U., and Kraemer, W.J. (1994). Developing explosive muscular power: implications for a mixed methods training strategy. Strength and Conditioning. 16(5): 20-31.

Reed, A., Ablack, D., and McNeely, E. (1992) Alactic Strength Training. SPORT 12(7).

Roth, W., Schwanitz, P., Pas, P., and Bauer, P. (1993). Force- time characteristics of the rowing stroke and corresponding physiological muscle adaptations.Int. J. Sports Med. 14 (suppl1):S32-S34.

Sale, D., and MacDougall (1981). Specificity in strength training; a review for the coach and athlete. SPORT . March 1981.

Salmons, S. (1994) Exercise, Stimulation and Type Transformation of Skeletal Muscle. Int. J. Sports Med. 15(3): 136-141.

Schmidt, R. (1991). Motor learning and performance: from principles to practice. Human Kinetics Publishers. Champagne, Ill.

Schmidtbleicher, D. (1985). Strength Training: Part 1 Classification of Methods. SPORT. August 1985.

Secher, N. (1993). Physiological and biomechanical aspects of rowing. Implications for training. Sports Med. 15(1): 24-42.

Secher, N. (1975). Isometric rowing strength of experienced and inexperienced oarsmen. Med. Sci. Sports. 7(4): 280-283.

Steinacker, J.M. (1993). Physiological aspects of training for rowing. Int. J. Sports Med. 14(suppl1):S3-S10.

Stone, M., and O'Bryant, H. (1987) Weight Training: A Scientific Approach. Bellwether Press, Minneapolis, Minnesota.

Verhoshansky, V.Y. (1986). Fundamentals of special strength training in sport. Sportivny Press: Livonia, Michigan.

Strength Training and Prepubescent Rowers

6

The number of children and adolescents participating in sports and weight training to prepare for specific activities (Blimkie, 1992) is on the rise. Traditionally, weight training had been discouraged for children because the safety and effectiveness of strength training in young athletes had not been established.

The prepubescent athlete is any athlete up to the age of 15 who has not yet developed secondary sexual characteristics (breasts, pubic hair, etc.) (National Strength and Conditioning Association 1985). The onset of puberty varies in individuals. Fifteen is reasonable as an upper estimate for the age of puberty, but an athlete may mature either before or after this age.

Strength Increases

One of the main reasons strength training has not been recommended for children stems from the debate as to whether prepubescent athletes can increase their strength through weight training. Vriejens (1978) found that prepubertal children did not increase their isometric strength following isotonic training. However, this study used only moderate training loads and the testing and training regimes were different. Docherty, Wenger, Collis and Quinney (1987) found small increases in isokinetic leg flexion (3.2% and 7.8%) and extension (2.25% and 2.0%) in boys 12.6 years of age after four and six weeks of resistance training. Several older European studies also found no significant strength increases in prepubertal subjects following training (Blimkie, 1993).

Many researchers have found that prepubertal children gain strength as easily as pubertal or post-pubertal athletes. Pfeiffer and Francis (1986) found significant increases in isokinetic strength in a group of nine- and 10-year-old boys following a period of traditional weight training.

Weltman et al. (1986) examined the effects of 14 weeks of hydraulic resistance training on isokinetic knee flexion, extension, and elbow flexion in prepubertal boys. They found strength increases between 18.5% and 36.6 % for both flexion and extension. The length of this study, the progressive nature of the training stimulus, and the similarity of the training and testing protocols strongly suggest that children can gain strength through resistance training (Blimkie, 1992).

Sailors and Berg (1987) found that eight weeks of free-weight training in a group of early prepubertal boys resulted in 52.3% increases in 5 RM squat, 19.6% increases in 5 RM bench press, and 26% increase in 5 RM arm curl.

In one of the longest strength training studies involving children (20 weeks), Ramsay et al. (1990) found significant improvements in 1RM bench press (34.6%) and leg press (22.1%). Part of the strength increase was attributed to growth. The control group increased strength by 12.3% on the bench press but it was significantly less than the experimental group. They also found significant increases in isokinetic and isometric peak torque for the knee extensors and elbow flexors. The study's training protocol was well designed; resistance was adjusted as the subjects became stronger. The testing protocol used specific and nonspecific testing that could have helped in controlling the learning effects.

Ozmun, Mikesky and Surburg (1994) studied boys and girls between the ages of nine and 12 who increased by 27.8% in isokinetic elbow flexion strength after eight weeks of dumbbell training three times a week. When the subjects could perform 11 repetitions the weight was increased. The training group's strength gains were 12.3% higher than those of the control group whose gains were attributed to growth.

The above studies (Ozmun, Mikesky and Surburg,1994; Ramsay et al., 1990; Sailors and Berg, 1987; and Weltman et al., 1986) provide strong evidence that pubertal and prepubertal subjects can significantly improve their strength through various forms of resistance training. Though some studies (Vriejens,1978; Docherty, Wenger, Collis and Quinney, 1987) reported no or small changes in strength, these studies were criticised for using modest training loads, lacking progressive resistance, using a low training volume or a short study duration (Blimkie, 1993). Although it appears that strength training, given sufficient intensity and duration of training, can improve strength in children, the mechanisms behind the changes are slightly different in children and adults.

Training Adaptations

In long-term strength training programs, the limiting factor for increasing strength is the ability of the body to adapt by increasing muscle size (Sale, 1992). However, strength performance is not only a function of muscle size. The ability of the nervous system to activate the muscles also determines strength (Sale, 1992). Moritani and DeVries (1979) showed that during the first four to six weeks of a new strength training program the adaptations are predominantly neural in nature. Their work also demonstrated that as hypertrophy becomes the main source of strength gains, neural adaptations detrain. These adaptations usually consist of improved motor unit activation through the recruitment of more motor units or more frequent activation of motor units, and greater synchronization of the firing patterns of the motor units (Sale, 1992).

In children, neural adaptations, not hypertrophy, seem to be responsible primarily for increases in strength (Blimkie, 1993). Ramsay et al. (1990), using computerized axial tomography, found no significant increases in muscle cross-sectional areas that could be attributed to training. They did, however, find an increase in the absolute

evoked twitch torque of elbow flexors and a trend towards an increase in the percentage of motor unit activation. Untrained individuals or those not accustomed to resistance training often cannot fully activate all their motor units (Sale, MacDougall, Upton and Comas, 1983).

Weltman et al. (1986) found insignificant increases in upper arm girth and triceps skinfolds. They attributed the increases to undefined neural adaptations. Sailors and Berg (1987) found a greater increase in the lean upper arm and calf areas of their control group than their training group. Vrijens (1978) found no increase in the upper arm and thigh cross-sectional areas of prepubertal subjects.

The use of EMG allows scientists to examine the level of motor unit activation during exercise. There is a higher EMG after strength training than before and the EMG increases correlate with the increases in strength (Moritani and DeVries 1979; Hakkinen and Komi, 1983; Hakkinen, Komi and Alen, 1985). Ozmun, Mikesky and Surburg , (1994) using IEMG found a 16.8% increase in neural activity following training in their group of nine to 12 year olds. There was no increase in IEMG in the untrained group.

Though improved motor unit activation is the most accepted theory of neural adaptation to strength training, it is not universally accepted. Rutherford and Jones (1986) using twitch superimposition to measure the level of muscle activation found that all their untrained subjects could fully activate their quadriceps while performing a maximal isometric contraction. They could not, however, measure the rate of motor unit firing using this technique. They attribute the adaptations in the first four to six weeks of training to improved coordination and the establishment of new neural pathways in the central nervous system. Blimkie (1993) also suggests that strength increases in children are in part due to improved coordination, especially in the complex multi-joint exercises.

Rutherford and Jones (1986) suggest that the neural adaptations occur because the muscle cannot generate sufficient force to stimulate hypertrophy until a certain degree of coordination is established. This is a plausible explanation since the rate of neural adaptation decreases throughout the strength training process as the rate of hypertrophy increases (Moritani and DeVries 1979; Hakkinen and Komi, 1983; Hakkinen, Komi, and Alen, 1985). The lack of hypertrophy in children following strength training may be due to lower levels of circulating androgens (Vrijens, 1978). Since the longest training study to date spans only 20 weeks (Ramsay et al. 1990), children may need longer training periods to experience significant hypertrophy.

Benefits and Risks

Strength training is often used to improve strength and sports performance in adults. Since many of the sports and activities that children participate in require significant strength and power, it seems appropriate to recommend resistance training to improve performance (Blimkie, 1993). The effects of strength training on performance can be difficult to measure because athletes are often involved in several different forms of training, all of which can affect overall performance. Weltman et al. (1986) found significant increases in vertical jump performance following strength training. There were also subjective reports of improved sports performance in the boys who trained. Even though there is likely a positive correlation between motor performance tests, like vertical jumping, there is no direct evidence that resistance training will improve athletic performance in prepubescent athletes (Blimkie, 1993).

The risk of injury associated with strength training greatly concerns many parents and coaches. According to a 1987 U.S. Consumer Product Safety Commission report, children between up to age 14 incurred 8,543 weightlifting injuries requiring emergency room treatment. Nearly 40% of these injuries were unsupervised. Inadequate supervision and an improper lifting technique most often cause strength training injuries in children (Blimkie, 1993; Mazur, Yetman and Risser, 1993).

Brown and Kimball (1983) conducted a survey of 71 adolescent competitive powerlifters and found that of the 98 injuries reported, 61% were muscle strains, the main site of injury being the lower back. Risser, Risser and Preston (1990) studied junior and senior high school football players and also found that the lower back was the main site of injury, and muscle strains were most common. Musculoskeletal injuries caused by strength training represent only about 0.66% of injuries reported in young football players (Mazur, Yetman and Risser, 1993). Although the most common strength training injuries are muskuloskeletal, the potential for damage to the growth plates of bones is the reason most often cited for not allowing children to strength train. Though the possibility of such an injury exists, concern is probably overstated (Blimkie, 1993). Only one case of a weightlifting induced epiphyseal fracture in prepubertal athletes has been reported (Gumbs, Segal, Halligan and Lower, 1982). When these injuries occur through strength training or other sports, there is rarely a detrimental effect on growth if the injury is diagnosed and treated properly (Caine, 1990).

This is further emphasized by the fact that there are virtually no injuries in the training studies involving children (Blimkie, 1993).

Although there is potential for injury during strength training, with proper technique and supervision strength training can help decrease the potential for certain types of injuries. Sports that do not involve the use of right and left sides of the body equally can result in bilateral strength imbalances that may be related to developing injuries (Knapik, Jones, Bauman and Harris, 1992). A strength training program designed to correct imbalances may help prevent these injuries. Cahill and Griffith (1978) and Hejna, Rosenburg, Suturusis and Krieger (1982) found strength training reduces the frequency and severity of injuries in high school athletes.

The benefits seem to outweigh the risks for children participating in resistance training. The potential for injury is lower for resistance training than many other sports, and strength training can improve performance and help prevent certain injuries making it an important element in preparing the young athlete. A child may carry a positive experience with weight training into adulthood, thus promoting a lifelong appreciation of fitness.

Recommendations

Based on the NSCA's position statement and reviews by Faigenbaum (1993), the American Academy of Pediatrics (1983), Blimkie (1993), and Israel (1992) the following guidelines for developing strength training programs for prepubescent children are recommended:

- Young athletes require a medical examination prior to strength training, including assessing their physical maturity level.

- Provide adequate supervision and instruction. The athlete-coach ratio should not exceed 10:1 with a ratio of 5:1 preferred. This should help the athlete learn proper technique. Most strength training injuries occur because of poor exercise technique.

- Prohibit maximal lifts. This helps prevent possible injury to a bone's growth zones. Since children and young teenagers are often competitive and want to see how much they can lift, it may be necessary to limit prepubertal athletes to very light weights

- Ensure the athlete is emotionally mature to accept and follow directions. Athletes risk injuring themselves and others when strength training if they cannot follow directions and safety guidelines.

- Consider the unique physical and psychological make up of each athlete. Since the rate of emotional and physical maturity varies from person to person, an individualized training program will help improve performance and decrease the chance of injury.

- Include strength training in a conditioning program. Expose young athletes to a variety of activities and movement patterns. Limiting training to a specific activity can slow the athlete's overall development.

- Keep training fun for the athlete. By keeping any training fun, the athlete can develop a lifelong appreciation of fitness and sport. The length of the athlete's career can be increased if the level of enjoyment is high.

- Develop or adopt a set of weight training rules and regulations.

- Create a periodized program to help avoid overtraining.

Program Design

1. Start with a four-week introduction period. During this time introduce the young athlete to the rules and regulations of the training facility. Use modified equipment or empty bars to initiate the athlete to exercise technique. During this period do not allow the young athlete to add weight to the bar until he or she can demonstrate relatively consistent exercise technique. One or two sets per exercise once or twice a week is sufficient.

2. During the next four to eight weeks emphasize improving exercise technique and start increasing the resistance. During this time

do not allow the athlete to use more than 60% of a 1RM. It has been suggested that variability in movement patterns increases with resistance above 60% of maximum (Schmidt, 1991). Keeping the resistance low should help the young athlete learn the movements more quickly. It is not necessary to train to failure with children. The repetition ranges should be six to eight with a maximum of 60% 1RM. This range should keep fatigue levels low enough to allow efficient skill learning. As the athlete becomes technically proficient, add weight to the empty bar or increase the number of sets. Increases in intensity or volume should not exceed 5% per week. Training should still be restricted to no more than two times per week and consider introducing weight circuits during this phase. Circuit training results in a random practice situation which has been shown to be more successful in skill teaching than blocked practice that occurs from a sets style of strength training.

3.   When the young athlete safely performs the basic exercises (multi-joint exercises) introduce higher training volumes and intensities. Training can increase to three times per week. Intensity can be increased to 70 to 75% of 1RM for three to four sets of six to eight repetitions. Again, emphasize that the young athlete not train to failure with this combination of volume and intensity.

References

American Academy of Pediatricians (1983). Weight Training and Weight Lifting: Information for the Pediatrician. The Physician and Sports Medicine. 11(3): 157-161.

Blimkie, C.J.R (1993). Resistance training during preadolescence issues and controversies. Sports Medicine. 15: 389-407.

Blimkie, C.J.R (1992). Resistance training during pre- and early puberty: efficacy, trainability, and persistence. Canadian Journal of

Sport Sciences. 17: 264-279.

Brown, E., and Kimball, R. (1983). Medical history associated with adolescent powerlifting. Pediatrics. 72: 636-644.

Cahill, B. and Griffith, E., (1978). Effect of pre-season conditioning on the incidence and severity of high school football knee injuries. American Journal of Sports Medicine. 6: 180-184.

Caine , D. (1990). Growth plate injury and bone growth: an update. Pediatric Exercise Science. 2: 209-229.

Docherty, D., Wenger, H., Collis, M., Quinney, H. (1987) The effects of variable speed resistance training on strength development in prepubertal boys. Journal of Human Movement Studies. 13:377-382.

Faigenbaum, A. (1993). Strength Training: A guide for Teachers and Coaches. National Strength and Conditioning Association Journal. 15: 20-29.

Gumbs, V., Segal, D., Halligan, J., and Lower, G. (1982). Bilateral distal radius and ulnar fractures in weight lifters. American Journal of Sports Medicine. 10: 375-379.

Hakkinen, K. and Komi, P.V. (1983). Electromyographic changes during strength training and detraining. Medicine and Science in Sports and Exercise. 15: 455-460

Hakkinen, K., Komi, P.V., and Alen, M. (1985). Effect of Explosive Type Strength Training on Isometric Force and Relaxation Time, Electromyographic and Muscle Fibre Characteristics of Leg Extensor Muscles. Acta Physiol. Scand. 125: 587-600.

Hejna, W., Rosenberg, A., Suturusis, D., and Krieger, A. (1982). The prevention of sports injuries in high school students through strength training. National Strength and Conditioning Association Journal. 4: 28-31

Israel, S. (1992) Age-Related Changes in Strength and Special Groups. In Strength and Power in Sport. An IOC Medical Commission Publication: Blackwell Scientific Publications. London: England

Knapik, J., Jones, B., Bauman, C., and Harris, J. (1992). Strength, flexibility and athletic injuries. Sports Medicine, 14: 277-288

Mazur, L., Yetman, R., and Risser, W. (1993). Weight training injuries, common injuries and preventative methods. Sports Medicine. 16: 57-63.

Moritani, T. and DeVries, H.A. (1979). Neural Factors Versus Hypertrophy in the Time Course of Muscle Strength Gain. , American Journal of Physical Medicine. 58(3):115-130.

National Strength and Conditioning Association (1985). Position Paper on Prepubescent Strength Training. NSCA Journal. 7(4): 27-31.

Ozmun, J., MIkesky, A., and Surburg, P. (1994). Neuromuscular adaptations following prepubescent strength training. Medicine and Science in Sports and Exercise.26: 510-514.

Pfeiffer, R., and Francis, R. (1986). Effects of Strength Training on Muscle Development in Prepubescent, Pubescent and Post Pubescent Males. The Physician and Sports Medicine. 14(9): 134-143.

Ramsay, J., Blimkie, C., Smith, K., Garner, S., MacDougall, J.D., and Sale, D. (1990). Strength Training Effects in Prepubescent Boys.

Med. Sci. Sports Exerc. 22(5): 605-614.

Risser, W., Risser, J., and Preston, D. (1990). Weight training injuries in adolescents. American Journal of Diseases of Children. 144: 1015-1017.

Rutherford, O.M., and Jones, D.A. (1986). The role of learning and coordination in strength training. Eur J Appl Physiol. 55:100-105

Sailors, M., and Berg, K. (1987). Comparison of response to weight training in pubescent boys and men. Journal of Sports Medicine. 27:30-36.

Sale, D.G. (1992). Neural Adaptations to Strength Training. In Strength and Power in Sport. P.V. Komi (editor), pp249-265. Blackwell Scientific Publications, London, England.

Sale, D.G., MacDougall, J.D., Upton, A.R.M., and McComas, A.J. (1983). Effect of strength training upon motoneuron excitability in man. Med. Sci. Sports Exercise. 15(1): 57-62

Sale, D.,and MacDougall, D. (1981). Specificity in Strength Training a Review for the Coach and Athlete. Canadian Journal of Applied Sport Sciences. 6: 87-92.

Schmidt, R. (1991). Motor Learning and Performance. From Principals to Practice. Human Kinetics. Champaign, Illinois.

Vrijens, F. (1978). Muscle Strength Development in the Pre-and Post-pubescent Age. Med. Sport. 11: 152-158.

Weltman, A., Janney, C., Rians, C., Strand, K., Berg, B., Tippitt, S., Wise, J., Cahill, B., and Katch, F. (1986). The Effect of Hydraulic Resistance Strength Training in Pre-Pubertal Males. Med. Sci. Sports Exerc. 18(6): 629-683.

Teaching Weight Training and Skill Development

7

Program design, periodization, and choice of exercises are are all important for the success of a strength training program. Teaching proper exercise technique is the most important thing a coach can do for a young rower. Good technique protects athletes from injury and allows them to eventually perform the exercises with heavy enough weight to optimize strength and power increases. Throughout this chapter, strength training sessions will be treated as practices and the movements will be referred to as skills. This is done to reinforce the idea that strength training exercises need to be treated in the same manner as any part of a rowing skill.

Many coaches and athletes talk about skill and the importance of high levels of skill for success in sport. Skill is also important in strength training. Improper technique is one of the main causes of injury in weight training. But, what exactly is a skill? E.R. Guthrie a noted psychologist has defined a skill as the ability to bring about some end result with maximum certainty and minimum outlay of energy, or of time and energy. In other words, skill is the ability to efficiently and effectively repeat a movement. This chapter is designed to introduce some fundamental concepts in skill learning and to provide some guidance for practice design.

Classification of Skills

Skills can be classified in several different ways.

Open and Closed Skills

Closed skills are skills where the environment, or opponents are predictable and will always react the same way. Open skills are those in which opponents or the environment can change and are free to interact with the athlete. Because weight training does not involve competition where your client has to react to a move an opponent makes. Weight training can be classified as a closed skill.

Discrete, Continuous and Serial Skills

Discrete skills are those which last for a short period of time and have distinct beginning and ending points. Throwing, kicking and jumping are all discrete skills. Continuous skills, running, swimming, cycling, have no particular beginning or end point. Many movements fall somewhere in between discrete and continuous skills. This large group of skills are known as serial skills. Serial skills can be thought of as a series of discrete skills strung together in a specific sequence to produce a new skill.

Motor and Cognitive Skills

Motor skills are those in which the quality of the movement determines the success of the performance. Cognitive skills are those in which a decision about a movement, rather than the quality of the movement, determine success.

The Stages of Skill Learning

There are three stages of skill learning that an athlete goes through from the time they are first introduced to a skill until they master it. These three stages are:

Verbal-Cognitive Stage

This is the first stage of skill learning. In strength training, this corresponds to children (or adults) who are working out for the first time. In this stage the problems of how to stand, where to look, where to put the hands, and many other basic concepts have to be learned. This stage lasts for a relatively short period of time (several weeks to a couple of months). The majority of this chapter will be dedicated to working with athletes in this group.

Motor Stage

This second stage of learning, focuses on developing more efficient and effective ways of performing a movement. Confidence improves and rapid progress can be seen in the early parts of this stage. This stage can last for a relatively long time (months).

Autonomous Stage

The third stage of learning, the autonomous stage, focuses on the development of automatic actions that do not require conscious attention. This stage is analogous to writing a program for a computer. Over a period of time, the motor program is written and modified until a simple cue action can trigger the automatic running of a complex movement program.

Teaching Skills to Beginners

Transfer of Learning

One of the objectives of practice is to transfer what is learned in the practice situation to the competition situation. Transfer of learning refers to how much learning one skill or situation can transfer to another. Transfer accounts for a large part of the learning that is done during the early stages of new skill development. For example, the descent into the bottom position of a squat is similar to sitting down on a low chair. By evoking this image in the athlete it may help them understand the descent in the squat.

Organizing a Practice

A number of factors should be considered when designing practices for beginners, these include:

Pre-Practice Preparation

As a coach it is important that you come to practice prepared to teach. Identify a number of skills that you want to teach. These skills should be organized from simple to complex. In the initial practices with a group of beginners the skills should involve a small number of joint movements and little coordination of the limbs.

Instruction

The type and complexity of instructions that are given before each drill can have a direct impact on skill learning. With beginners and young children long descriptions of a skill will probably not be understood. Instructions should be kept very simple. For example, "keep your head up" is more effective with beginners than "keep your head tilted slightly so that your eyes are focused 45 above the horizon."

People are capable of learning through observation and imitation. Demonstrations can be a very powerful learning tool for beginners. Often, the best instruction for beginners is "Do this" followed by a demonstration. It is important for coaches to have a good understanding of the movement patterns of their own and other sports. In order to facilitate transfer of learning, the coach should use examples of how weight training skills are similar to other more common movement patterns that have probably already been learned.

Feedback

Feedback is extremely important during all stages of skill learning. If done properly, feedback motivates an athlete, supplies reinforcement for good performances and provides a basis for correction of errors. During the earliest stage of learning, feedback is required frequently. Ideally, it should be given following almost every trial of a skill. Feedback should be positive and directed at the movement pattern rather than the result of the movement. Be specific and directed at changing one fault at a time. Example: Nice lift. The starting position looked pretty good but, next time keep your hips lower.

Special Considerations for Young Lifters

Rate of Progression

The rate at which an athlete can develop a skill will depend upon many factors, some of which the coach can't control. In young children, physical maturity, which proceeds at a genetically determined rate, is a major factor over which a coach has no control. Fitness level can affect skill learning. If the athlete is not strong enough or flexible enough it may be impossible for them to maintain or assume crucial positions. Coaching style can affect skill learning. If a coach is a poor communicator, or lacks fundamental knowledge of weight training, it will make it very difficult for the athlete to learn a skill.

What Should be Practiced?

Coaches of young children are faced with a dilemma, what should be coached? It is important that young children experience a variety of movements and activities for proper physical development. However, by exposing the child to a wide variety of activities, you are taking away from time that could be used to teach sport-specific activities. A wide variety of activities will allow a child to develop the levels of strength, flexibility, and endurance that will be useful in learning specific skills. In pubertal children or older, the emphasis should be placed upon sport-specific training since there is little evidence that general training with these people will benefit sport-specific performance.

Frequency of Practice

One of the main concerns for every coach is how often should people practice. Ideally, an athlete should practice as often as possible. However, it is important to remember that the rate of progress in learning a skill will be negatively affected by fatigue. If inadequate time is left between training (both physical training and skill training) sessions progress in skill learning will be slow. For the type of training that is typically done by the general population, three to five skill training sessions per week will allow enough time between training sessions for physical recovery. For younger children, one to three skill sessions per week will allow adequate physical recovery.

Duration of Practice

The duration of practice will be dependent upon the physical demands of the drills and skills that are taught. Higher intensity drills (jumping, sprinting) will force the practices to be relatively short (possibly less than one hour).

Types of Practice

Whole vs. Part Practice

Some weight training movements are a series of complex skills. In teaching these movements, a coach must decide whether to teach whole movement, or if the individual components of the performance should be taught separately (part practice).

Part practice is based on the idea of transfer of learning. The goal is to have the learning of individual parts transfer to the performance of the complete skill. Part practice can be used if one component of a skill can be easily separated from others. In some movements this may seem relatively easy.

The first pull, second pull, squat under and squat skills of a clean can be easily separated from one another. Part practice can be very useful in teaching these skills to athletes of intermediate ability. However, the ability to perform a good clean is dependent not only on the individual skills, but on the interaction of these skills. Whole skill learning has to be done in order for the proper interaction of the skills to be learned.

In summary, whole practice needs to be done for beginning lifters. Part learning will form the majority of practice time for intermediate ability lifters (they should also be exposed to some whole-skill practice), and whole-skill learning is necessary for advanced lifters to perfect the interactions between the skills. However, they still need some part learning for refinement of the individual components of the lift.

Random vs. Blocked Practice

Traditionally, during a practice an athlete will work on one skill for a period of time and then move on to another skill. This is called block practice because the skills are practiced in independent blocks. There seems to be a certain logic about practicing in this manner, it allows the athlete to concentrate on one thing at a time. Unfortunately, this does not seem to be the most effective way of teaching a skill.

Random practice, is practice where work on different skills is mixed throughout the practice. This type of practice appears to be more effective in the long term for learning a skill. Shea and Morgan were the first to discover this phenomena in 1979. They found that when skills were learned under blocked practice the subjects showed greater acquisition (the were able to perform the skill better at the end of the practice) of the skill than under random practice conditions. However, when asked to perform the same skill several days later, the subjects who had learned the skill under random practice conditions performed much better than those who had learned with blocked practice. This means that even though it may look like an athlete is improving during practice they really are not learning the skill.

Random practice seems to be more effective for learning a skill because the athlete is given the opportunity to forget. In blocked practice the athlete has the opportunity to remember how to do the task from one trial to the next. They only have to generate the new movement pattern once. In random practice, when a second movement is introduced it replaces the first pattern in the athletes short term memory. When the athlete comes back to the first movement they are forced to generate the movement pattern again. The act of regenerating the movement pattern seems to speed up the learning process.

Timing and Accuracy

In training for power, the timing and accuracy of the lift are critical for good performance and safety. Timing and accuracy can be developed like any other skill. In order to understand what has to be done to teach timing the physical basis of timing must be understood.

Kinesthetic Feedback

Kinesthetic feedback refers to the feedback that the body provides about its position and motion. The feedback about body position, and balance is provided predominantly by four systems; the muscle spindles, the Golgi tendon organs, the vestibular system, and the visual system. These systems work together in providing information to the brain, which ultimately controls movement and movement changes.

The muscle spindles are stretch sensors that consist of nerve endings wrapped around modified muscle fibres. The spindles can sense when and how much a muscle contracts. The signals that are produced by the spindles are returned to the central nervous system – the brain and spinal cord – where they are used to help modify a movement. This ability to sense changes in a stretch allow the spindles to act as sensors for subtle changes in body position (this helps in the maintenance of proper balance).

Golgi Tendon Organs

Golgi tendon organs are found near the junction of tendons and muscles. Tendon organs provide feedback about the amount of tension that is being placed upon a muscle.

The Vestibular System

The vestibular system refers to the semicircular canals in the inner ear. These fluid-filled canals provide information about the position of the head. The vestibular system is crucial for balance.

The Visual System

The visual system provides feedback on stability and balance, and velocity of movement. There is an emerging field of sport optometry dedicated to the training of visual processes to help athletes perform better.

The processes by which these systems are integrated and controlled within the brain are quite complex and beyond the scope of this chapter. Although these systems are crucial for the development of timing and accuracy, it is still not clear whether the function of these systems, with the exception of the visual system, are trainable. It is known however, that athletes can become more focused on the feedback that these systems provide. This improved focus can play an important role in the development of timing.

Training for these systems involves both mental and physical processes. The athlete has to become aware of the different sensations they experience during a lift. Drills such as broomstick simulations blindfolded can help the athlete develop their kinesthetic senses for lifting. Setting up a safe practice area is very important if you plan on trying this.

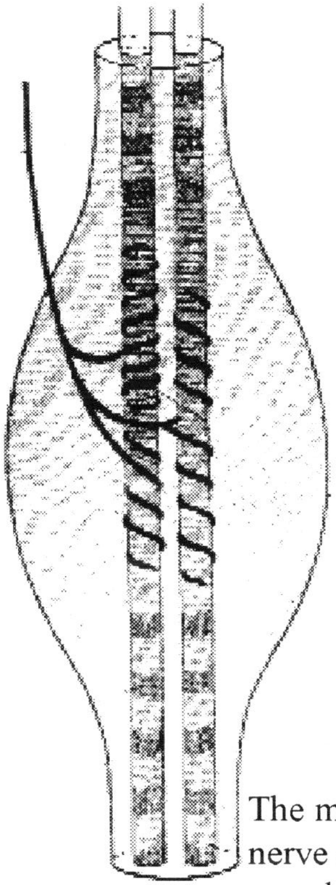

The muscle spindle is a
nerve end and modified
muscle fibres

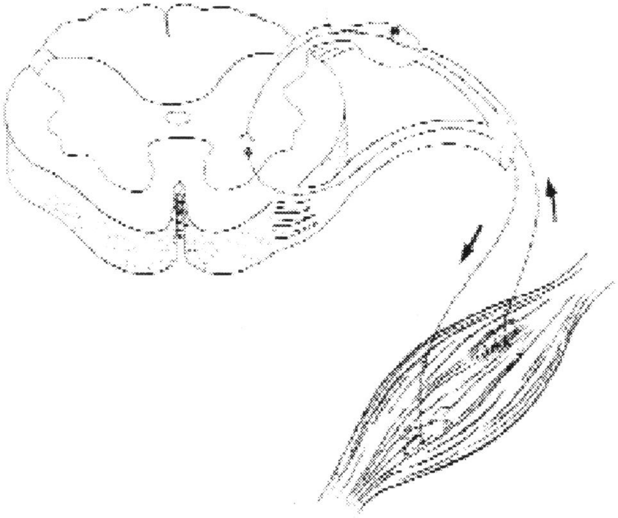

The spindle is connected to the
spinal cord and feeds back onto
the muscle fibre itself

Designing an Exercise Technique Program

Program design will have a major impact upon the rate at which the athlete learns to do the exercises. The number of sets and reps, rest, recovery, and selection of exercises will all influence rate of learning.

Sets and Reps

Training to failure is common among people who strength train. There is no evidence that training to failure results in improved strength or muscle size (Stone et al. 1996). There are several reasons why regularly training to failure may do more harm than good.

The metabolic fatigue that results in the failure point has been found to interfere with the ability to learn a task (Benson, 1968; Carron and Ferchuk, 1971; Carron, 1972; Carron and Thomas, 1972). Normal activation of motor units is compromised during fatigue. Performances under fatigued conditions force the recruitment of more type II fibres to try to maintain the work load. This probably results in the generation of motor patterns that are unique from the non fatigued patterns (Berger and Smith-Hale, 1991). Because of the specificity required in skill learning the patterns developed during fatigue result in a less than optimal rate of skill acquisition (Berger and Smith-Hale, 1991). In addition, the changes in movement pattern that occur during fatigue could lead to injury.

In order to avoid the learning problems caused by fatigue, a set should be stopped as soon as any sign of technical failure occurs. In other words, as soon as technique becomes inconsistent the set should be stopped. Another way of doing this is to have the athletes do three less reps than they are physically capable of. If the athlete

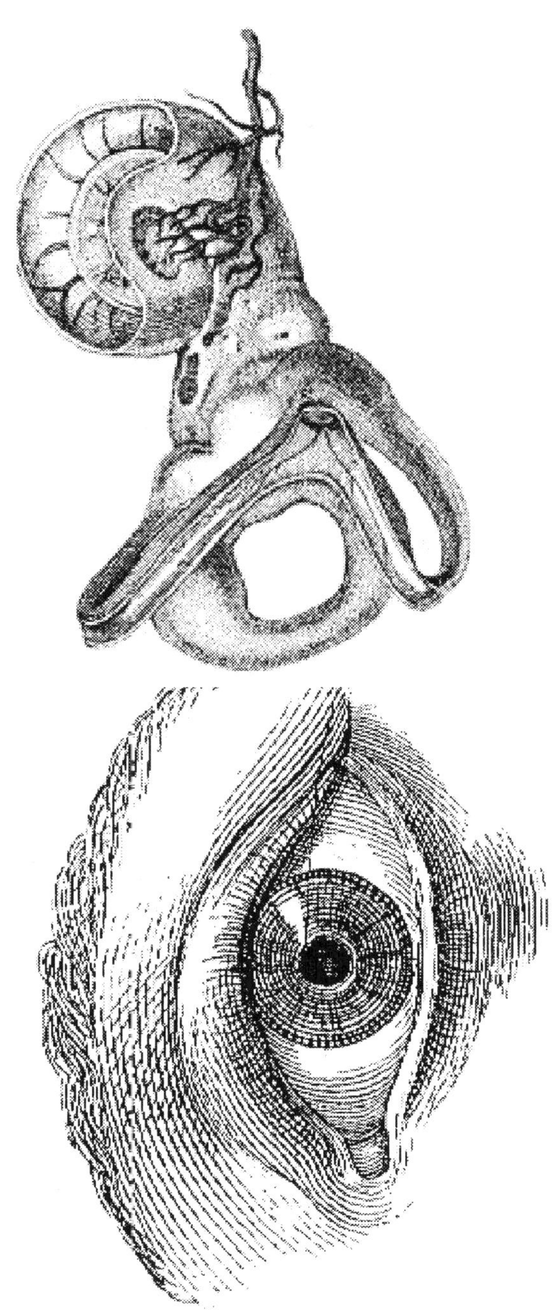

The visual and vestibular (inner ear) systems are not only crucial for feedback in skill development but they are of primary impor- tance in the development of balance

153

is using a weight they could lift 15 times they should stop at 12 repetitions.

Rest and Recovery

Rest refers to the period of time between each set or exercise, and recovery is the period of time between training sessions. The objective of rest and recovery is to minimize the impact of fatigue on performance and learning.

The main energy system used in strength training is the anaerobic alactic system. This system uses the stored ATP and CP in the muscles for energy. The alactic system can be used for 10 to 15 seconds of work before it is depleted. Sets that last longer than 15 seconds result in lactate accumulation. Lactate is responsible for fatigue and impaired skill learning. Full recovery of the alactic system can occur in about three minutes. Full recovery helps prevent lactate accumulation and fatigue.

Intensity

Intensity refers to the amount of weight lifted and is expressed as a percentage of the maximum weight lifted (1RM). Learning strength exercise technique should be done at intensities of less than 60% of 1RM (this is a weight they could lift approximately 15 times).

Selection of Exercises

In the first year of training athletes should be exposed to a wide variety of exercises. The most common mistake that coaches make is to emphasize only rowing specific exercises. Since rowing performance during the first year is going to improve mostly by improved rowing technique there is no need to emphasize rowing specific strength work. Exercises for muscle balance and stability should be as important as rowing specific exercises.

Besides the available equipment the choice of exercises should be based upon your ability to demonstrate the exercises. It will be difficult for the athlete to learn an exercise if they do not have a model to copy. Learning how to do the exercises properly should be of primary concern for all coaches. If you do not know how to do an exercise, it should not be in the program.

Circuit versus Traditional

Circuit training refers to performing a series of exercises with no rest in between. Traditional strength training involves a set of repetitions followed by a rest period followed by repeating the same exercise. Circuit training is most effective when teaching exercises (random practice). The circuit should be set so that upper and lower body exercises are alternated.

Conclusion

Weight training exercises are no different than any other sport skill. The processes that go on in the brain are no different for learning a basketball free throw and learning a squat. Trainers need to pay more attention to motor learning concepts in order to help their athletes learn exercise techniques in the fastest, most efficient manner.

References

Benson, D. (1968). Influence of imposed fatigue on learning a jumping task and a juggling task. Res. Quart. 29: 251-257.

Berger, R., and Smith-Hale, L. (1991). Effects of fatigue on performance and learning of a gross motor task. J. Appl. Sport Sci. Res. 5(3): 155-161.

Carron, A., and Ferchuk, A. (1971). The effect of fatigue on learning and performance of a gross motor task. J. Motor Behavior. 3: 62-68.

Carron, A. (1972). Motor performance and learning under physical fatigue. Med. Sci. Sports Exerc. 4: 101-106.

Carron, A., and Thomas, J. (1972) Temporary fatigue effects in a gross motor skill. J. Motor Behavior. 4: 217-222.

Stone, M., Chandler, J., Conley,M., Kramer, J., and Stone, M. (1996). Training to muscular failure is it necessary?. Strength and Conditioning. 18(3): 44-48.

Flexibility Training

8

Flexibility is defined as the range of motion (ROM) available at a joint. Flexibility is specific to each joint; that is, a person may have a large ROM at the wrist joint in all directions, but a limited ROM in the shoulder. Flexibility is important to athletes for three reasons: Injury prevention, skill development and performance, and power production.

Flexibility and Injury Prevention

The information available on flexibility and injury prevention is inconclusive (Hubley-Kozey, 1991). Several prospective studies have found that athletes with higher flexibility levels had lower rates of injury (Ekstrand and Gilquist, 1983; Lysens et al. 1989). Unfortunately, it is impossible to determine if flexibility was the only contributing factor to the lower injury rates in some athletes in these studies.

Stretching before exercise does not appear to decrease the rate of injury (Calder, 1999). Stretching after training significantly lowers injury rates (Calder and Sayers, 1992; Hartig and Henderson, 1999). However, developing too much flexibility can result in joint laxity and increase the risk of injury.

Flexibility and Skill Development

Consistency of movement is a key factor in skill development (Schmidt, 1991). If the athlete cannot achieve the required range of movement for a skill they will not be able to learn the skill. In high-level athletes many technical errors are the result of inadequate strength or flexibility. It is only by correcting this problem that such errors can be eliminated.

Flexibility and Power Production

In rowing, power and boat speed can only be increased while the oar is in the water. Greater flexibility allows the oar to be in the water for a longer amount of time. However, flexibility is only one part of the power production equation. If the athlete is too flexible, he or she may over reach and actually decrease power production at the catch. The muscles are at a mechanical disadvantage in an extreme stretched position.

Types of Flexibility

There are two main types of flexibility – active and passive. Passive stretching involves an outside source creating the movement. This outside source may be a partner, a machine, momentum or gravity. The athlete may be active during passive stretching. An example of passive stretching occurs when an athlete uses dumbbells to go through a greater range of motion in the bench press than they could with no weight or a barbell. While the athlete is active the stretch is passive because the weight is forcing the athlete through the range of motion (ROM), the athlete is not pulling the arms through the full range. There is a slight risk of injury in passive stretching if the motion is pushed too far (Alter, 1988).

Active stretching involves the individual moving to a position of slight discomfort and holding this position before releasing. Active flexibility is the ROM available when internal muscle forces cause the movement range. If a segment must be moved through a range by the muscles, weakness in those muscles may cause the ROM to be less than what it would be passively. Holt and Smith (1982) report differences averaging 18 degrees in hip flexion ROM in favor of passive flexibility.

Factors Affecting Flexibility

There are a number of factors that influence flexibility these include joint structure, age, body type, disease or injury and inactivity. ROM is joint specific; it depends on the structure of the joint. For example, a ball and socket joint, such as the shoulder, has a greater ROM than a uni- or biaxial joint, such as the knee (Heyward, 1984). The joint capsule is said to account for 47% of a joint's total resistance to movement.

The more active an individual, the greater ROM that individual has. In inactive people, the connective tissue shortens with disuse and restricts the joint's movement. The areas of the body in which large movements of the segments are neglected will exhibit the greatest movement restriction or inflexibility. This is not a permanent situation and can be improved by following flexibility or stretching programs or by increasing activity (Winslow-Germain, 1983). Habitual movement patterns of an individual are also important. The joint and surrounding tissues adapt to the same movements. Using the joints and muscles in the same activity pattern or maintaining habitual body postures may restrict range motion owing to the tightening and shortening of the muscle tissue (Heyward, 1984). This is similar to the inactive individual and the situation can be corrected with more and varied activity.

Gender plays a role in flexibility. Evidence suggests women have greater flexibility than men (Winslow-Germain, 1983). The female is designed this way, especially in the pelvic region, to assist in pregnancy and childbirth. Women tend to have lighter and smaller bone composition that allows greater movement (Alter, 1988). Women also tend to have smaller and less-defined muscles, thus allowing freer range of movement (Heyward, 1991).

Age is a major contributor in flexibility performance. Stiffness and immobility may result from at least three factors: true aging changes, an increasingly sedentary lifestyle, and unrecognizable disease processes (Winslow-Germain, 1983). Saxon and Etten have shown that muscles have less elasticity and flexibility with age (Winslow-Germain, 1983). As one grows older, muscle atrophy also occurs. Muscle fibres are replaced by fatty tissue. These changes are partly responsible for decreased flexibility (Alter, 1988). A second explanation for decreased flexibility is an inactive lifestyle. Many people become less active with age. Exercise is an effective means of altering performance declines resulting from age (Rikli, 1991). However, by increasing activity patterns, flexibility can be improved. The decreased levels do not have to be permanent (Winslow-Germain, 1983). For some older individuals, undetected diseases set in. These diseases hinder ROM and may cause discomfort to the individual. An example of this is osteoarthritis, the most common musculoskeletal problem in the elderly. There is therapy available, but the results are not guaranteed (Alter, 1988). Vandervoort et al (1991) studied ankle flexibility in men and women age 55 to 85. As the subjects got older, flexibility significantly decreased. They concluded that flexibility exercises should be incorporated into fitness programs for seniors.

The age factor also plays a role in developing children. A study by Alexander, Lindner and Black (1991) have concluded that rapid bone growth can increase muscle-tendon tightness around the joints and inhibit ROM. This occurs because the muscles do not grow as fast (Alter, 1988). There is also the possibility that the attachments grow faster than the bones. This results in hypermobility; which can remain throughout life or improve as the child continues to grow (Alter, 1988).

Body type, in this instance, refers to tendons, ligaments, muscle fascia, skin, and other connective tissues. Bone, muscle, ligament and joint capsule, tendon, and skin determine the range of motion for any joint (Humphrey, 1981). A study by Johns and Wright (1962), determined that tendons and ligaments provide 10% of the total resistance experienced by a joint during movement. Muscle and its fascia account for 41% and skin accounts for 2%. Muscle and facia is composed of more elastic tissue and is therefore better in reducing resistance to movement and increasing dynamic flexibility. However, excess fatty tissues and large, hypertrophied muscles may hinder movement (Heyward, 1984).

Collagen, fibrous connective tissue, and elastin, elastic tissue, are also determinants. The dominating tissue in a joint area, helps in determining its relative ROM. The elastic tissues give greater flexibility as compared to the fibrous tissue (Alter, 1988). Because connective tissue is the target for flexibility programs, understanding the response of connective tissue to stretching, or elongation, is important. When connective tissue is elongated, its lengthening has two components: elastic stretching (it will recoil) and plastic stretching (it will not recoil). The permanence of the stretch depends on how much plastic stretch occurs; the elastic-type lengthening merely causes recoil of the tissue to its original length. The plastic elongation is directed toward the viscous (thick fluid) property of the viscoelastic nature of connective tissue. The proportion of the contribution of each kind to the lengthening depends on how the stretching is performed. The three variables concerned are; the magnitude of the stretching force, the duration of the stretching force, and the tissue temperature when the stretching is taking place (Sapega et al. 1981). Summarizing the information provided by Sapega et al., permanent lengthening of connective tissue is produced best by lower force of longer duration applied at elevated tissue temperatures (40 °C or 104 °F and above in therapeutic settings). Cooling the tissue (by ice packs about 15 min) before releasing the tension seems to increase the permanence of the plastic elongation. In addition, under these conditions, structural weakening of the tissues is minimized. Elastic lengthening (elongation that will recoil) is produced by high-force, short duration stretching at normal or colder tissue temperatures.

Injuries and diseases are also determinants of ROM. Scar tissue may be movement-inhibiting because it is less compliant than undamaged tissue (Hubley-Kozey, 1991). The onset of disease, such as osteoarthritis, may produce pain, thus limiting an individual to find relief as opposed to movement (Alter, 1988).

Methods of Stretching

Stretching methods are categorized as static or dynamic. Static stretching is also known as passive or slow, sustained stretching. Dynamic stretching is called active ballistic, bouncing, or fast stretching. Research studies on flexibility improvement indicate that both methods are effective but that static methods are safer and result in less muscle soreness (deVries 1980, Corbin and Noble 1980, Bealieu 1981, Holt and Smith 1982).

Dynamic Stretching

Dynamic stretch of a muscle group brings into play neuromuscular mechanism involving the muscle spindle (myotatic, or stretch reflex) and the Golgi tendon organ. In fast stretching, the momentum of the moving body segment, rather than an external force, is used to push the articulation beyond its present ROM. Dynamic stretching is important for sports which require high speed running, jumping, throwing or striking movements. For example, in baseball a pitcher's throwing arm stretched beyond its active range on motion by the momentum generated through the hips and trunk. Training ballisticly is the most sport-specific way of improving shoulder flexibility for these athletes.

The speed of stretch elicited by the dynamic method stimulates the muscle spindles, and the stretch reflex causes a contraction of the same muscles that are being stretched. The greater the speed of muscle stretching, the greater the stretch reflex. Therefore, even though

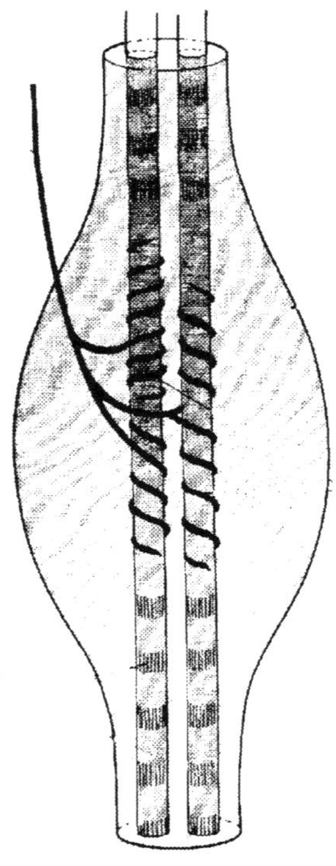

Figure 1. The muscle spindle is a modified muscle fibre that is sensititve to changes in the amount and rate of stretch placed on the muscle.

the momentum brings the articulation beyond its normal range, the ballistic method causes a countercontraction immediately following or during the stretch and seems to reduce stretching benefits. Reports associate muscle soreness with this type of stretching; that is, before motion stops, the sudden tension put on the tissues can result in small tears in the connective tissue or muscle fibers, which lead to swelling or pain.

This is very similar to what happens during plyometric training. Since there is no plyometric component to the rowing stroke(even the transition from recovery to catch is too slow to be plyometric) dynamic flexibility is not necessary for rowers.

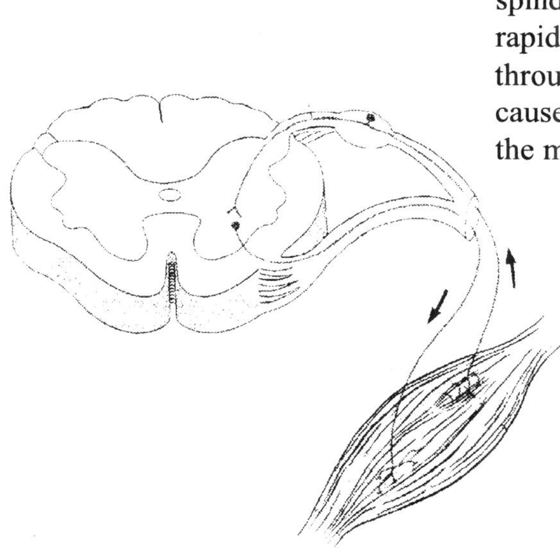

Figure 2. When the muscle spindle is activated by a rapid stretch a signal is sent through the spinal cord that causes a reflex contraction of the muscle that was stretched

Static Stretching

Static stretching is the most common form of stretching. It involves assuming a stretched position and holding it for a period of time. To reduce the velocity of stretch that the muscles undergo and thus reduce the intensity of the stretch reflex, an external object, such as a wall or a partner, or an antagonistic muscle group is used to apply tension slowly to the muscles to be stretched and thus causes these muscles to stretch beyond the normal range. Some muscle-spindle activity results from the stretched position, but it is minimal because the spindles react more to the speed of stretch than to the stretched position.

In light of the properties of connective tissue, the static, or long duration low force, methods are safer alternatives to ballistic stretching (unless ballistic stretching is sport specific). In addition, an easy muscle warm-up activity prior to stretching increases the plastic elongation of the tissues due to the increase in temperature. Sapega et al. (1981) propose that stretching exercises not be done at the beginning of a warm-up routine. Stretching should be performed immediately after the main part of a workout because it is then that the tissue temperatures are the highest. There is some current research suggesting that, in speed and power sports, static stretching should be avoided during the warm up. Static stretching has been shown to decrease strength by up to 7% in the immediate post-stretch period (Calder, 1999).

Proprioceptive Neuromuscular Facilitation

The proprioceptive neuromuscular facilitation (PNF) method of stretching in various forms is gaining acceptance (Corbin and Noble 198C, Moore and Hutton 1980, Salem 1980, Holt and Smith 1982). Reports indicate that the ROM of an articulation may be increased considerably by this method and that little soreness results. PNF is also referred to as CRAC (contract-relax with agonist contract). PNF stretching involves a passive movement to the onset of stretch followed by a maximal isometric contraction against resistance before passively moving further into the range of motion. The contraction is held for four to 10 seconds followed by four to 10 seconds of relaxation before moving.

PNF training can be done alone or with the aid of a partner. Because PNF exercise is potentially dangerous (especially when performed improperly) communication between the subject and the partner is essential. In order to keep PNF stretching safe, the following guidelines for communication should be followed:

- The person being stretched (the subject) is in charge and controls how much they are to be stretched
- The person doing the stretching (the partner) should maintain a

strong stable body position. This will prevent slipping or falling when the contraction is performed.

- The partner must make sure the joints are properly aligned. Forceful contractions in poorly aligned joints can lead to injuries.
- The subject should tell the partner when they are going to begin the contraction.
- The partner acts as an object that the subject pushes against. The partner should never push against the subject.
- The partner should immediately remove all stretch from the subject if they are told to.
- When trying to increase the range of motion following the contraction do so slowly.
- The subject should increase the force of the contraction slowly. Starting with a maximal contraction can throw the partner off balance.
- Try to relax the muscles surrounding the joint during the stretch.

Planning a Flexibility Program

What to Stretch

The decision as to what stretches should be done must be based on an analysis of the athlete. Technical errors need to be analyzed to determine if they are caused by flexibility problems. Body symmetry should be tested to determine if there is a flexibility imbalance between the right and left sides. Flexibility training should only be done for joints that are inflexible. Improving flexibility in an already flexible joint may create an instability and increase the chance of injury.

Which Type of Stretching

The type of stretching used (static, ballistic, PNF) depends on the demands of the sport. In rowing, either static or PNF is appropriate because there are no ballistic movements in the sport. In wrestling, PNF is more appropriate because the athlete is often isometrically contracting muscles while under extreme stretch. For sprinters ballistic flexibility would be most important through the ankles and hips. Each type of stretching has value in specific circumstances. PNF and ballistic stretching should not be dismissed as dangerous forms of exercise because of biases developed by the fitness industry, which is geared toward sedentary, untrained people.

Frequency of Stretching

If the stretching program is not overly aggressive, stretching can be done every day. Ballistic stretching and PNF sometimes result in muscle or joint soreness the day after the session. If this is occurring the athlete should wait three to four days before the next session.

Duration of Stretch

There has been quite a bit of debate over how long a stretch should be held. Currently it is believed that the most important factor is the total stretch time and not the duration of a single stretch. In order to most effectively improve flexibility, a total of 60 seconds of stretch time needs to be done for each movement in the program. For instance, three stretches of 20 seconds each produce a total stretch time of 60 seconds. Six stretches for 10 seconds each also produces a total stretch time of 60 seconds.

When to Stretch

Stretching during a warm up does not prevent injury nor does it increase flexibility. Static stretching during a warm up may even decrease performance in strength and power activities. Stretching during a warm up is primarily to help establish the existing range of motion and enhance technical skills. To improve flexibility stretching should be done after a training session. When muscle temperatures are high the muscles are more elastic and receptive to stretching.

References

Alexander, M.J.L., K.J. Kindner and B. Black.(1991) Strength and Flexibility Development in Relation to Physical Growth During Puberty. Proceedings of the 24th Annual Meeting of the Canadian Association of Sport Sciences (CASS). Kingston, October 1991.

Alter, Michael J. Science of Stretching. Champaign: Human Kinetics Books, 1988.

Beaulieu, E. (1981) Developing a Stretching Program. The Physician and Sports Medicine 9 (11): 59-69.

Calder, Angela., (1999). Flexibility- A key training and performance factor. Strength Summit proceedings from Investors Group International Coaching School. Victoria, B.C.

Calder, A., and Sayers, M. (1992). Testing and improving flexibility. Sports Coach. 15(2): 7-12.

Corbin, C. B., and Noble, L.(1980). Flexibility, a Major Component of Physical Fitness. "JOHPER
51 (1): 23-24, 57-60.

deVries, H. A.(1980). Physiology of Exercise. 3d ed. Dubuque, Iowa: William C. Brown Co.

Ekstrand J, Gillquist J, Moller M, Oberg B, and Liljedahl S, (1983)

Incidence of soccer injuries and their relationship to training and team success. American Journal of Sports Medicine, 11: 63-67.

Hartig D E, and Henderson J M, (1999) Increasing hamstring flexibility decreases lower extremity overuse injuries in military basic trainees. The American Journal of Sports Medicine, 27 (2): 173-176.

Heyward, Vivian H. Advanced Fitness Assessment & Exercise Prescription. 2nd Edition. Windsor: Human Kinetics Publishers, Inc., 1991.

Heyward, Vivian H. Designs for Fitness. Minneapolis: Burgess Publishing Company, 1984.

Holt, L. E., and Smith, R. K. (1982). The Effect of Selected Stretching Programs on Active and Passive Flexibility. In Biomechanics in Sports: Proceedings of the International Symposium of Biomechanics in Sports, ed. J. Terauds, 54-67. Del Mar, Calif.: Research Center for Sports.

Hubley-Kozey, Cheryl L. "Testing Flexibility." Physiological Testing of the High-Performance Athlete. Second Edition. Champaign: Human Kinetics Books. pp.309-359, 1991.

Humphrey, Dennis L. "Flexibility." JOPERD. pp.41-43, September 1981.

Knapik, Joseph J., Bruce H. Jones, Connie L. Bauman and John McA. Harris. "Strength, Flexibility and Athletic Injuries." Sports Medicine. 14(5):277-288, 1992.

Kreighbaum, Ellen and Katharine M. Barthels. Biomechanics.3rd Edition. New York: MacMillan Publishing Company,   1990.

Lysens R J, Ostyn MS, Auweele YV, Lefevre J, Vuylsteke M, and

Renson L, (1989) The accident-prone and overuse profiles of the young athlete. American Journal of Sports Medicine, 17: 612-19.

Moore M A, and Hutton R S, (1980) Electromyographic investigation of muscle stretching techniques, Medicine and Science in Sport and Exercise 12:322-329.
Rikli, Roberta E. and Diane J. Edwards. (1991). "Effects of a Three Year Exercise Program on Motor Function and Cognitive Processing in Older Women." Research Quarterly for Exercise and Sport. 62(1):62-67   1991.

Salem, N. (1980). Selected Stretching Techniques Based on Mechanical and Neurophysiological Principles and Muscle Tightness. In Biomechanics: Proceedings of the Biomechanics Symposium, ed. J. M. Cooper and B. Haven, 352-53. Indiana State Board of Health.

Sapega, A. A., Quedenfeld, T. C., Moyer, R. A., and Butler, R. A. (1981). Biophysical Factors in Range of Motion Exercise. The Physician and Sportsmedicine 9 (12): 57-65.

Schmidt, R. (1991). Motor Learning and Performance. Champaign: Human Kinetics Books

Vandervoort, A.A., B.M. Chesworth, D.A. Cunningham, D.H. Paterson, P.A. Rechnitzer and J.J. Koval. "Effect of Age on Ankle Muscle Strength and Flexibility." Proceedings of the 24th Annual Meeting of the CASS. Kingston, October 1991.

Winslow-Germain, Nancy and Steven N. Blair. "Variability of Shoulder Flexion with Age, Activity and Sex." American Corrective Therapy Journal. 37(6):156-160, 1983.

Tapering

9

During the final preparation for a major competition, the athlete needs to feel rested, quick, and strong. To accomplish this, a taper is often used. A taper is a period of drastically reduced training volume that lasts from seven to 21 days prior to the year's major competition (Costill et al., 1985; Houmard and Johns, 1994). Unfortunately, there are no published studies on tapering and rowing performance. This is partially because changing wind and water conditions make it difficult to do accurate pre- and post-taper measures on competitive rowers. Therefore, much of the information used by rowing coaches and scientists comes from swimming, cycling and running.

The objective of training is to induce physiological and mechanical changes in an athlete so that their performance improves. During periods of high-volume training common to rowers training adaptations are often masked by the fatigue of incomplete recovery between sessions (Zatsiorsky, 1995)(figure 1). The main purpose of a taper is to allow the physiological systems to completely recover and adapt. In order to plan a taper training volume, intensity, frequency, and duration all need to be considered.

Volume

In studies of distance runners, (Houmard et al., 1990, 1991) found that 800m and 1600m running times were improved following a decrease in training volume of 70% over a three-week period. Houmard (1994) found an increase in running economy and a 3% improvement in 5km run time following a seven-day 85% decrease in training volume. If training volume is not sufficiently reduced there appears to be no improvement in performance. Sheply et al. (1992) looked at the effects of a seven-day 62% reduction in volume and compared it to a seven-day 90% reduction in volume. They found the 62% scenario did not increase the time to exhaustion. On the other hand the 90% reduction resulted in an 22% increase in

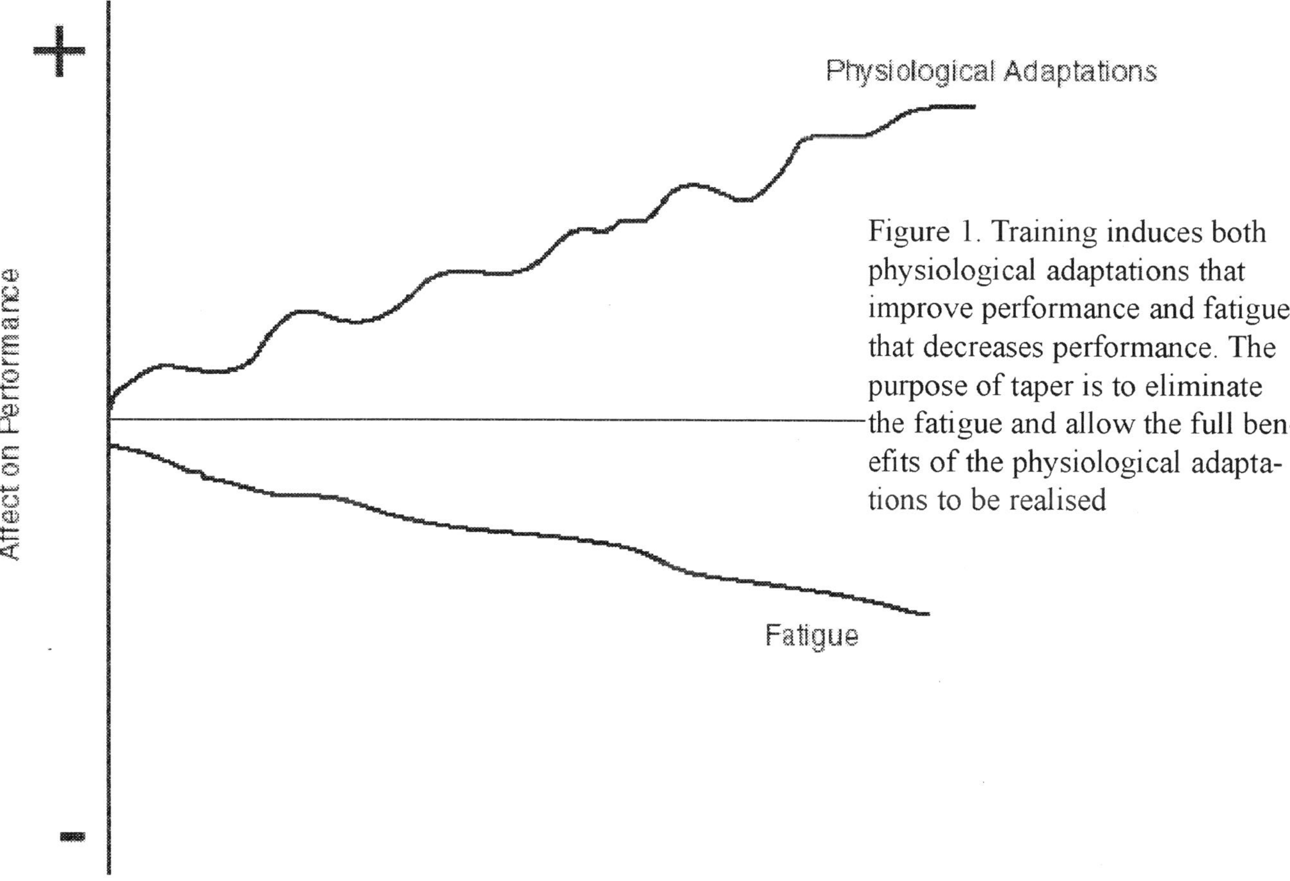

Figure 1. Training induces both physiological adaptations that improve performance and fatigue that decreases performance. The purpose of taper is to eliminate the fatigue and allow the full benefits of the physiological adaptations to be realised

time to exhaustion. A 40-day taper in which training volume was reduced by 76% resulted in a 2.8% increase in swim performance (Johns et al. 1992). Mujika et al. (1995) found there is a significant relationship between the amount of volume decrease and performance improvements during a taper. From the available data, it appears that reductions in training volume of 70 to 90% are necessary for a taper to be most effective.

A taper can either be progressive, meaning there is a gradual decrease in volume over the period of the taper, or it can be stepped, meaning there is a single decrease in volume for the duration of the taper (Mujika, 1998). Martin et al. (1994) found that performance improvements peaked during the first week of a two-week step taper in cyclists. Zarkadas et al. (1994) found an 11.8% improvement in 5km run times following a 10-day progressive taper but only a 3% improvement in performance using a step taper. Houmard et al. (1990) found no improvement in performance following a three-week step taper. Progressive tapers seem to have a greater impact on performance than step tapers (Mujika, 1998). This is probably due to detraining effects that occur when the rapid volume decrease used in step tapering is maintained for an extended period of time. While a progressive taper is the obvious choice for the major competition of the year, a step taper may be better for qualifying competitions and other less important events where the taper duration is much shorter.

Frequency

Training frequency refers to the number of training sessions per week. The reduction of training volume in a taper should not occur as the result of drastic changes in training frequency (Houmard and Johns, 1994). Neufer et al (1987) found that reducing training volume (80 to 90%) through cutting frequency by 50 to 85% resulted in decreased swim power after only seven days of tapering. Studies in which tapering has resulted in improved performance have typically decreased frequency by 20 to 50%. Houmard et al. (1989) has recommended that training frequency not be reduced by more than 20%. The reasons why a reduction in frequency causes a decrease in performance is unclear, but may be related to decreased technical efficiency. As frequency of technical work is decreased there is probably some loss in technique that ultimately affects performance.

Intensity

Intensity during a taper is usually maintained or increased. There is a tendency for a greater proportion of the training to become race-specific type intervals. In rowing, this translates into increased training in categories III and II. The time period between the intervals should be long enough to maximize intensity. Hickson et al. (1985) reduced training intensity by 66% and found that cycling time to exhaustion decreased by 21%. In a study that compared high intensity and low intensity tapers Shepley et al. (1992) found that the physiological responses to the two tapers were similar but only the high intensity taper group showed an increase in performance. Houmard and Johns (1994) suggested that training schedules that use intensities of less than 70% VO_2 max maintain, or decrease performance during a taper, while schedules which use intensities of greater than 90% VO_2 max improve performance. The higher intensity training allows athletes to get used to higher stroke rates, allows them to work on race strategy and tactics, and psychologically give them feelings of speed and power.

Duration

Since the training stimulus is greatly reduced during a taper, the duration of the taper can have an impact on the magnitude of performance improvements. Within one to four weeks of stopping training highly trained athletes start to show decreases in performance

(Costill et al. 1985). Mujika et al. (1996) studied the effects of 21-, 28- and 42-day tapers on performance in highly trained swimmers. They found significant improvements in the 21- and 28-day groups but not the 42-day taper group. Several studies have looked at physiological changes associated with tapering and found that haemoglobin and hematocrit peaked after seven days of taper (Yamamoto et al. 1988). Studies that have measured performance and taper duration have found improvements in performance following tapers of seven to 21 days (Costill et al. 1985; Houmard et al, 1994; Sheply et al. 1992).

The number of days needed to taper may be affected by training volume and intensity going into the taper and fitness level of the athlete. Mathematical models have been developed to try and predict the optimal number of days needed to taper (Mujika et al., 1996; Fitz-Clarke et al., 1991; Morton et al., 1991). The models have suggested that tapers should not be longer than 16 days. However, there have been discrepancies between the mathematical models and measured performance peaks. More time is needed to validate these models before they can be used with complete confidence. As a general rule the taper duration should be a function of the competitive level of the athlete. Lower level athletes can get away with a seven-day taper while national level rowers need a 14- to 21-day taper.

Special Considerations During a Taper

The taper period can be a time of high psychological stress for both the coach and athlete. Coaches tend to worry about the training that was done during the season, the duration of the taper, and many other things that arise prior to a major competition. It is important at this time of the year that the coach projects confidence both in what has been done during the season and in the taper. If the coach is openly worried about the athlete's preparation or starts making changes to a planned taper the athletes may begin to question their

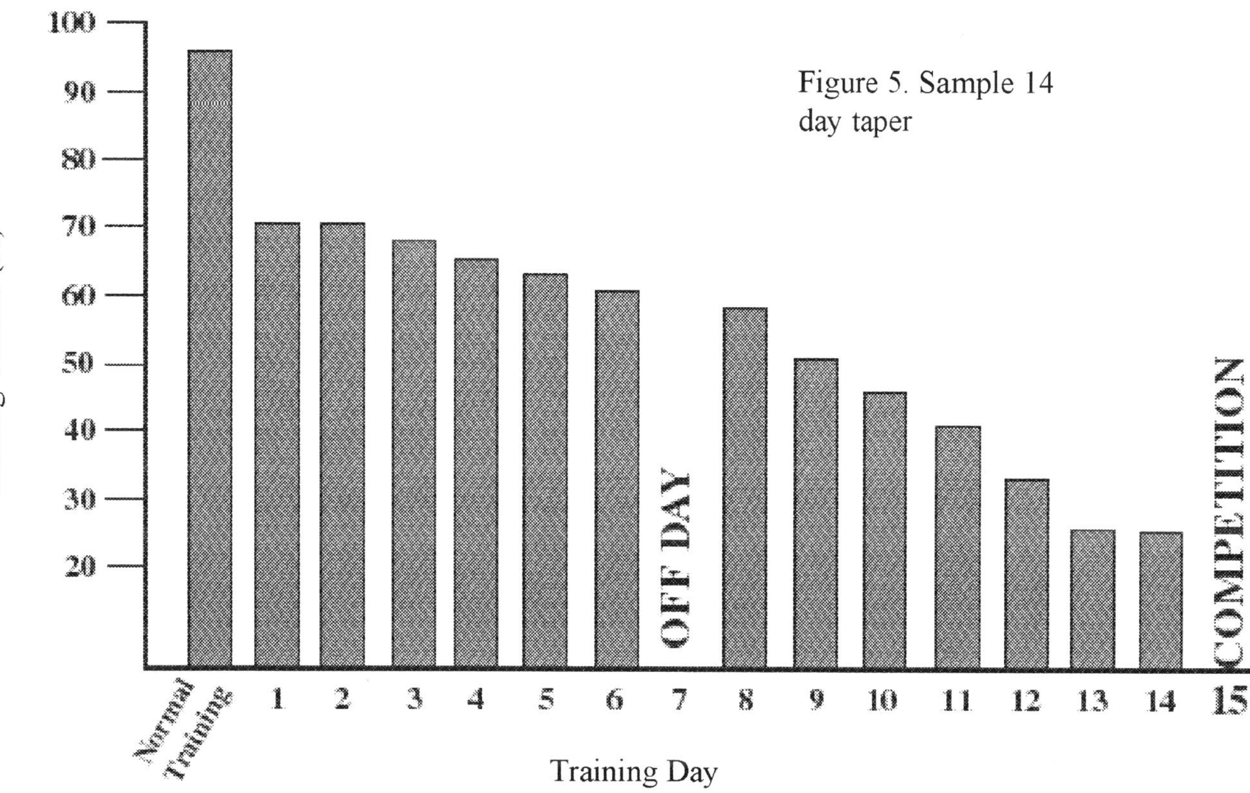

Figure 5. Sample 14 day taper

preparedness and ability to win.

Athletes handle the decreased training volume differently. Many athletes will enjoy the feelings of speed, power and renewed energy. Others have a tough time dealing with the decrease in volume. They worry about detraining and don't know how to cope with the extra time as a result of the decreased volume. A coach needs to be aware of the responses of each athlete, and be prepared to deal with the worriers.

Lightweight rowers need to pay attention to their weight during a taper. One of the adaptations to a taper is an increase in muscle glycogen storage (Sheply et al. 1992). For every gram of glycogen stored in the muscle three grams of water are stored. This can result in a large increase in weight in a relatively short period of time. A certain amount of weight gain may be necessary if the athlete is to see performance improvements as a result of the taper. The increased glycogen storage not only feeds the muscles during training but it is used as an energy source for other adaptations to occur. Lightweight rowers have to carefully balance the amount of glycogen supercompensation that will improve performance with the amount of weight they can gain.

Conclusion

A well-designed taper can improve performance by about 3% over the year's best performance. The taper should involve a progressive decrease in training volume of 70 to 90% and an increase or maintenance of training intensity over a seven- to 21-day period. The decreased training volume should be accomplished by decreasing distance or time per session. The number of training sessions per week should not be reduced by more than 20 to 50%.

References

Costill, D., et al. (1985). Metabolic characteristics of skeletal muscle during detraining from competitive swimming. Med. Sci. Sports Exerc. 17: 339-343.

Fitz-Clarke, J., et al. (1991). Optimizing athletic performance by influence curves. J. Appl. Physiol. 71: 1151-1158.

Hickson, R., et al. (1985). Reduced training intensities and loss of aerobic power, endurance, and cardiac growth. J. Appl. Physiol. 58: 492-499.

Houmard, J., et al. (1989). effects of reduced training on submaximal and maximal running responses. Int. J. Sports Med. 10: 30-33.

Houmard, J., et al. (1990) Reduced training maintains performance performance in distance runners. Int. J. Sports Med. 11: 46-52.

Houmard, J., et al. (1994). The effects of taper on performance in distance runners. Med. Sci. Sports. Exerc. 26: 624-631.

Houmard, J. (1991). Impact of reduced training on performance in endurance athletes. Sports Med. 12: 380-393.

Houmard, J. and Johns, R. (1994). effects of taper on swim performance: Practical implications. Sports Med. 17: 224-232.

Johns, R., et al. (1992). Effects of taper on swim power, stroke distance and performance. Med. Sci. Sports Exerc. 24: 1141-1146.

Martin, D., et al. (1994). Effect of interval training and taper on cycling performance and isokinetic leg strength. Int. J. Sports Med. 15: 485-491.

Morton, R., Fitz-Clarke, J., and Banister, E. (1990). Modelling human performance in running. J. Appl. Physiol. 69: 1171-1177.

Mujika, I. (1998). The influence of training characteristics and tapering on the adaptation in highly trained individuals. Int. J. Sports. Med. 19: 439-446.

Mujika, I., et al. (1996) Modelled response to training and taper in competitive swimmers. Med. Sci. Sports Exerc. 28: 251-258.

Mujika, I. et al. (1995). Effects of training on performance in competitive swimmers. Can. J. Appl. Physiol. 20: 395-406.

Sheply, B., et al. (1992). Physiological effects of tapering in highly trained athletes. J. Appl. Physiol. 72: 706-711.

Yamamoto, Y. et al (1988). Hematological and biochemical indices during the taper period of competitive swimmers. In Ungerects et al (Eds) Swimming Science V, International series on sports sciences. 18: 243-249. Human Kinetics Books, Champaign Ill.

Zarkadas, P., Carter, J., and Banister, E. (1994). Taper increases performance and aerobic power in triathletes. Med. Sci. Sports Exerc. 26: 34

Zatsiorsky, V. (1995). Science and Practice of Strength Training. Human Kinetics. Champaign Ill.

Nutritional Ergogenics and Rowing

10

Athletes are always looking for an edge over the competition. They experiment with different training methods, oars, boats, and rigging. Many athletes also resort to nutritional manipulations to enhance performance. There are more than 600 different nutritional preparations available that claim to have some sort of health or performance-enhancing effect.

Unfortunately, most of theses preparations have either not been tested or have received very little human testing. Often those that have been tested have only been tested by the manufacturer and the results have not been duplicated in an impartial laboratory. Many athletes may be wasting money on supplements that do not deliver what they promise.

In addition to issues about whether or not a supplement works, there are ethical issues to be considered before supplements are taken. Each coach or athlete is faced with the decision about using supplements to enhance performance. The IOC has a general definition of doping that states that "any physiological substance taken in abnormal quantity with the intention of artificially and unfairly increasing performance should be construed as doping" (Williams, 1998). While this obviously includes anabolic steroids and other drugs on the IOC banned substance list the spirit of the definition of doping could just as easily include nutritional supplements. This can lead to ethical dilemmas for some coaches and athletes. Many will decide that if it isn't specifically named as a banned substance it is acceptable for use in competition. Others will feel that artificial enhancement of performance destroys the integrity of the competition.

This chapter describes specific nutritional supplements that are in use by rowers and may improve performance. The legality of the supplements will be discussed, but no judgement will be made as to the ethics of using nutritional supplements to enhance performance.

Sodium Bicarbonate

Individuals in high-intensity anaerobic activities have tried to use sodium bicarbonate as a means of delaying fatigue and maintaining high power output.

The Role of Sodium Bicarbonate

During high-intensity anaerobic activity lactic acid levels increase rapidly. As lactic acid levels increase muscular fatigue sets in and performance decreases. This performance decrease is the result of a drop in intramuscular pH, brought about by an increase in hydrogen ion concentration (H+).

Sodium bicarbonate is an alkaline salt found naturally in the body. Sodium bicarbonate is broken down in the body and the bicarbonate ion that is formed is used in the buffering of lactic acid. This can be seen in the equation below.

$$H^+ + HCO_3^- \longrightarrow H_2O + CO_2$$

The goal of supplementing sodium bicarbonate is to increase the amount of bicarbonate in the body. The increased bicarbonate is supposed to increase the buffering capacity and decrease the affects of lactic acid. This is proposed to delay fatigue and improve performance.

Sodium Bicarbonate Supplementation

Muscle cell membranes are impermeable to (bicarbonate) HCO_3^-. Increases in extracellular (outside the cell) HCO_3^- has no effect on intracellular (inside the cell) pH. However, there does appear to be an increase in the rate at which lactate is transported out of the cell as a result of sodium bicarbonate ingestion. Several well controlled studies suggest that sodium bicarbonate supplementation can increase performance, and decrease the psychological discomfort associated with high-intensity anaerobic exercise. The ingestion of sodium bicarbonate increases the time to fatigue by an average of 27%. There is no increase in maximal power associated with this supplement.

Both the duration of exercise and the dosage of sodium bicarbonate need to be considered when assessing the effectiveness of supplementation. Exercise sessions that last less than one minute or more than seven minutes do not benefit from sodium bicarbonate supplementation. Dosages of around 300 mg/kg of body weight have been found to be the most beneficial. Highly trained athletes tend to benefit less from supplementation than lesser trained athletes or untrained individuals.

Adverse Effects

The long-term effect of sodium bicarbonate ingestion is unclear. Possible side effects are thought to be due to the sodium content of the supplement. Increased water retention and high blood pressure are often attributed to sodium ingestion. For this reason, sodium bicarbonate supplementation should not be recommended to individuals with cardiovascular problems that may be aggravated by increased blood pressure.

The short-term side effects of sodium bicarbonate loading may negate any of the benefits of the supplement. These include gastrointestinal discomfort, diarrhea, cramps, bloating, and dehydration. The side effects occur primarily with larger doses and can often be relived by drinking water during and after the supplementation. Very high doses could lead to alkalosis which causes apathy, irritability, and muscle spasm.

Legal Issues

Sodium bicarbonate is currently legal for use by athletes. Athletes involved in drug testing should note that the ingestion of sodium bicarbonate may lead to alkaline urine. An alkaline urine sample may mask some banned substances. During a drug test an athlete who passes a highly alkaline sample will probably be detained until an acidic urine sample is provided.

Recommendations

Based on the current scientific evidence sodium bicarbonate supplementation does appear to improve performance in events where a maximal effort is required for one to seven minutes. A dosage of 300 mg/kg of body weight, taken with lots of water seems to be effective and safe.

Creatine

In recent years creatine supplementation has become very popular with elite athletes, bodybuilders, strength trainers and the general public. There have been hundreds of studies done to examine the effects of creatine supplementation on strength and power improvements. Unfortunately, there are only a few studies on the effects of creatine on sport performance.

Creatine Production

About 95% of all creatine in humans is found in skeletal muscle (Balsom, Soderlund and Ekblom, 1994). Fast twitch fibres tend to have a higher content of creatine than slow twitch fibres (Tesch, Thorsson and Fujitsuka, 1989; Soderlund, Greenhaff and Hultman, 1992). The larger creatine pool, along with differences in myosin heavy chain type, partially explains why fast fibres are better at high speed and power activities than slow fibres. A diet consisting of meat, fish and other animal products supplies approximately half of the daily requirement for creatine, which is about 1g for the average male (Hoogwerf, Laine and Greene, 1986). The body synthesizes the rest of the daily requirement. Three different amino acids; glycine, arginine and methionine form creatine. Enzymes in the liver, pancreas, and kidneys help the chemical reactions needed to transform these amino acids into creatine (Balsom, Soderlund and Ekblom, 1994). The amount of creatine synthesized in these organs seems to depend on the amount consumed (Walker, 1960).

The Role of Creatine

Creatine plays a major role in producing energy. Adenosine triphosphate (ATP) is the source of energy for working muscle. During exercise ATP is broken down and must be replenished. Creatine, in the form of creatine phosphate, plays a role in replenishing ATP (see formula below).

1. ATP $\longrightarrow$ ADP
2. ADP + Crphos $\longrightarrow$ ATP + Crfree

Various studies estimate that high-intensity or all-out exercise could deplete creatine phosphate stores within 10 seconds. This depletion is considered a limiting factor in maintaining force output during high-intensity exercise (Balsom, Soderlund and Ekblom, 1994) and is partially responsible for the failure experienced during strength training.

During submaximal aerobic activity creatine phosphate levels also decrease (Broberg and Sahlin, 1989) but not to as great an extent as in high-intensity exercise (Balsom, Soderlund and Ekblom, 1994). Creatine is, however, not likely the major contributor to fatigue.

Creatine supplementation

Humans supplement creatine levels by ingesting creatine monohydrate powder dissolved in a liquid (Balsom, Soderlund and Ekblom, 1994). Harris et al. (1992) found that supplementation could increase creatine phosphate storage in the muscles by more than 20 per cent. This increase also results in an increase in body weight which is probably due to water retention (Balsom, Soderlund and Ekblom, 1994) or, as some studies suggest, to slight increases in lean body mass (Kreider, 1995).

Some studies found that creatine supplementation increased performance of repeat anaerobic bursts. Greenhaff et al. (1993) found subjects improved knee extensor torque during five sets of 30 repetitions with 60 seconds rest between sets after five days of ingesting creatine. Balsom et al. (1993) found that creatine supplementation improved their subjects' performance of repeated six-second bicycle sprints at a target intensity. Soderlund, Balsom and Ekblom (1994) used a cycling protocol similar to Balsom et al. and found that creatine supplementation significantly improved subjects ability to sustain a high power output during a 10-second work bout. They also found that muscle lactate accumulation following the final work bout was 70 % lower after supplementation.

Part of the theory behind creatine use is that it increases the ability to recover from strength- and power-training sessions (Plisk and Kreider, 1999). Several studies have shown there is a greater improvement in strength or power performance when training is done using creatine (Kirskey et al 1999; Peeters, Lantz, and Mayhew, 1999; Pearson, Russel, and Harris, 1998).

Creatine use has also been shown to increase performance in sports requiring repeated sprint-type efforts. It has been shown to improve sport-specific performance in baseball players but not basketball players (Lefavi et al. 1998). This may be because basketball is more continuous in nature and requires more of an aerobic energy contribution than baseball. Other studies have looked at physiological changes in athletes but have not used true performance measures to assess the effectiveness of creatine.

Creatine supplementation does not appear to improve endurance performance. Balsom et al. (1993b) found no improvement in the time to complete a 6 km cross-country course. The group that used the creatine supplement performed worse than the group that used placebos. The poor performance may have been due to the supplemented group's weight increase. There are currently no studies on the effects of long term creatine use on endurance performance.

Only one study has looked at the effects of creatine supplementation on rowing performance. Rossiter et al. (1996) found that after a five-day supplementation period, performance time on an all-out, 1000m Concept II B test improved time by an average of 2.3 seconds. The most significant changes occurred in the final 400m of the test. To date there has been no research done on the effects of creatine supplementation on on-water performance or on a 2000m ergometer performance.

Balsom, Soderlund and Ekblom (1994) proposed three methods whereby creatine supplementation may improve performance:

• a higher pre-exercise concentration of creatine phosphate,
• a smaller decrease in muscle pH, and
• a higher rate of resynthesis during recovery.

These mechanisms share one major objective: decrease the time that anaerobic glycolysis occurs in energy production and decrease the negative impact that decreasing pH can have on high intensity performance.

Adverse Effects

Supplementing creatine to improve performance is relatively new. Few studies have attempted to examine the actual or potential side effects of this supplement. There appear to be no side effects when dosages are used for less than two weeks (Balsom, Soderlund and Ekblom, 1994). Creatine feeding is believed to suppress the natural production of creatine by interfering with transamidinase activity (one of the enzymes responsible for synthesizing creatine). Whether this suppression is lifted once creatine feeding is terminated is currently unknown in humans. Even if it does return to normal, how long it takes to do so is not known. Any time delay between the end of a supplement cycle and the resumption of normal creatine production could potentially have a negative impact on performance.

Practical Implications for Rowers

Creatine supplementation may help athletes improve their performance in sports where the availability of creatine phosphate may be limited. Athletes who sprint, cycle and swim would likely benefit most from supplements (Balsom, Soderlund and Ekblom, 1994). The increase in body weight associated with supplementation, however, may counter any benefits gained. While there may be some improvement in ergometer performance, increasing the weight in the boat also increases the drag on the boat.

This weight gain should be of particular importance to lightweight rowers who have difficulty making weight. The amount of weight gained seems to be individual and unpredictable. If lightweights are to use creatine supplements they should experiment with it prior to the competitive season.

Creatine Dosages

There are usually two phases to creatine usage. A loading phase where 20g of creatine are taken every day for five days. A maintenance phase where 5g of creatine are consumed every day.
Since little is known about the possible side effects of creatine supplementation, creatine should be cycled. It can be used for four to eight weeks with two to three weeks off.

Legal Issues

Creatine supplementation looks promising as an ergogenic aid. Currently, it is not a banned substance.

Recommendations

Creatine supplements have not been shown to increase performances in events of six- to eight-minute duration. There is no reason to believe that rowing performance will be enhanced as a result of creatine supplementation and it may even be decreased in crew boats if the weight gain of the crew increases the drag on the boat. Lightweights in particular should be careful if using creatine.

Glutamine

Glutamine is potentially one of the few nutritional supplements that will work for athletes trying to improve or maintain their muscle mass. Glutamine may potentially have it's largest effects during a pre-competition phase of preparation, or a bout of dieting for lower body fat levels. Glutamine is used to control many homeostatic functions of various tissues in the human body. (Rowbotton et al., 1996) Two of the most important functions are those of the gut and the immune system. The skeletal muscle reserves of glutamine are responsible for supplying these tissues with extra glutamine under times of stress. (Rowbotton et al., 1996)

Exercise that places a holistic stress on the body will change the homeostasis in the body. During high-intensity exercise, plasma levels of glutamine are seen to increase, with a significant decrease in plasma levels, post exercise. Several hours may be needed to see plasma levels return back to normal (Rowbotton et al., 1996). The accumulated effects of lowered levels of glutamine may be a result of inadequate recovery time between workouts. These levels may remain chronically low for months, even years if this environment continues. Glutamine supplementation may therefore play a role in maintaining the body's muscle mass, through an anti-catabolic effect on the muscle.

Glutamine Metabolism

Glutamine is known to be a neutral amino acid which is found in very high levels in skeletal muscle and plasma. There are two principal enzymes responsible for glutamine production and metabolism in the body. Glutaminase, and glutamine synthetase are responsible for maintaining a relatively constant level of glutamine during resting periods. (Damian, 1970) Glutamine, once formed in the body is responsible for many things. These include transfer of oxygen between organs, detoxification of ammonia (Newsholme, 1983), maintenance of acid base balance during acidosis, (Damian, 1970, Goldstein, 1980, Pitts, 1972), being a nitrogen precursor for the synthesis of nucleotides (Krebs,1980), a fuel for the mucosal cells of the gut and the immune system (Hanson, 1977, Souba et al., 1985, Windmeuller, 1974, 1975), and possibly a direct regulator of protein synthesis and degradation (MacLennan, 1987).

Whole body exchange rates of glutamine, have been seen to exceed the body's stores several fold. The major supplier of glutamine in this situation is the skeletal muscle. This of course can create a deficit within the skeletal muscle which may lead to unnecessary catabolism. This mechanism may be mediated through an increase in glucocorticoids such as cortisol, due to resistance training. The skeletal muscle is the organ of primary synthesis with the lungs, brain, liver and possibly adipose tissue all contributing as well. It is estimated that glutamine levels are approximately 20 mmol/L of intracellular water (Bergstom, 1974). Glutamine is also responsible for approximately 60% of the free amino acid pool in the body. The average free amino acid pool in the human body is around 70 grams, approximately 40 grams of which is glutamine (Sauba, 1992). Glutamine stores are seen to be as much as three times higher in slow twitch muscle fiber then in fast twitch muscle fiber. These stores are know to be the major contributor to the needs of other tissues (Newsholme, 1990). Consequently many other organs rely on the contribution of glutamine by skeletal muscle, leaving the muscle with lower levels on a regular basis.

Adding glutamine in supplement form, may not increase the skeletal muscle stores but may supply the other organs (especially the gut) with the needed glutamine consequently leaving skeletal muscle levels much higher. Strength training may also produce the effect of lowered glutamine levels in skeletal muscle for upwards of six days (Keast et al., 1995), and supplementation may offset this training effect as well.

Adverse Effects

Supplementing glutamine has been seen to be safe and effective in raising skeletal levels of glutamine. There does not appear to be any adverse effects to taking glutamine supplements. However, more research needs to be done to determine the long-term effects supplementation in humans.

Legal Issues

Currently glutamine supplementation is not banned by the IOC.

Recommendations

Glutamine may be a useful and safe method of maintaining muscle mass particularly for lightweight rowers trying to make weight. Take in three servings of two to three grams of glutamine each day, with one serving before bedtime during periods of very high training volume or weight reduction.

Caffeine

Caffeine is both a nutritional ergogenic aid and a pharmacological ergogenic (Williams, 1998) and seems to be a favorite among lightweight rowers. Caffeine is used by athletes for a variety of reasons. As a central nervous system stimulant, caffeine increases psychological arousal and may help athletes wake up for early morning training sessions.

Caffeine has been used in diet pills as an appetite supressant. Even small doses of caffeine (100 mg) can increase metabolic rate (Friedl, 1992). This may be useful for lightweight rowers trying to make weight.

Caffeine has been shown to have performance enhancing effects on long duration endurance events (Costill et al, 1978; Friedl, 1992; Graham et al, 1994) but not shorter duration events. The time to fatigue has been seen to increase by up to 51% as a result of caffeine ingestion (Graham et al. 1994). The exact mechanisms through which caffeine increases performance are not known. The theory is that caffeine increases the release of a group of hormones called catecholamines which increase fat mobilization and utilization. Since carbohydrate stores are one of the main limiting factors in endurance performance, the ability to use more fat spares the carbohydrate stores allowing them to last longer (Williams, 1998; Graham et al, 1994).

Table 1. Caffeine content of some common foods

Food/Beverage	Caffeine (mg/serving)
Coffee (250 ml)	
Brewed	60-90
Instant	75-125
Drip	95-150
Tea (250 ml)	
Strong	60-75
Weak	40-50
Cola (375 ml)	40-50
Chocolate (50 g)	10-15
Excedrin	65
No Doz	100
Vivarin	200

Since a rowing race is usually eight minutes or less, caffeine will probably have very little positive effect on race performance. Increased catecholamine levels increase lactate levels. Since lactate accumulation is the major cause of fatigue over a 2000 m race artificially increasing lactate levels by using caffeine may decrease rowing performance. However, caffeine use may help athletes cope long training sessions and large volumes of work.

Adverse Effects

Many investigations have attempted to link long-term caffeine ingestion with various types of cancer and heart disease (Tarnopolsky,
1994). More work needs to be done in this area, but currently there
is little evidence that caffeine increases the risk for developing these
diseases.

There are several short term side effects of caffeine that may
decrease performance. Caffeine ingestion close to bed time can dis-
rupt sleeping patterns decreasing total sleep time, deep sleep (where
recovery occurs), and result in daytime sleepiness. This can impact
the quality of workouts and increase the likely hood of overtraining.

Caffeine is a diuretic. Increased water loss may put the athlete at
greater risk for dehydration and heatstroke. It is recommended that
one cup of water is consumed for every 100mg of caffeine to help
eleviate these problems. When rowing in hot and humid weather, it
is often difficult to maintain hydration without increasing the problem through caffeine use.

Caffeine ingestion has been shown to increase anxiety, restlessness,
muscle tension and tremor. These side effects can impact the athletes
mental preparedness and technical performance. Similar symptoms
have been seen with withdrawal in habitual users (Tarnopolsky,
1994).

Legal Issues

Caffeine has been on and off the IOC banned substance list for
years. It was originally added to the list in 1962 and removed in
1972. Currently, it is classified as a restricted drug when urine levels
are greater than 12 mg/L of urine. The USOC has found that 100 mg
of caffeine produces a urine profile of 1.5 mg/L. Doses of 800 mg or
more will result in a positive test (Williams, 1998).

There is little evidence that caffeine ingestion will benefit rowing performance. Its carbohydrate sparing effect may help with long training sessions, and it may be of benefit to lightweights when they are making weight. If caffeine is used dosages should be kept to 5 mg/kg of bodyweight or less. This dosage can provide ergogenic effect without causing a positive drug test (Williams, 1998).

Vitamin/Multivitamin Mineral Supplements

Vitamins and minerals are involved in almost all metabolic processes in the human body as well as recovery and adaptation (Burke and Read, 1993). They are needed for the formation of red blood cells, muscle protein, neurotransmitters, and antioxidant activity (Williams, 1998). Vitamins and minerals have been marketed as performance enhancers for all types of activities.

The intake of vitamins or minerals in excess of the RDA/RNI (Recommended Dietary Allowance/ Recommended Nutrient Intake) has not been shown to increase performance (Belko, 1987; Burke and Read, 1993; Williams, 1998). However, if there is a nutritional deficiency supplementation up to the RDA/RNI can improve performance. If a rower is consuming an adequate number of calories from a variety of food sources their vitamin and mineral intake is well in excess of the RDA/RNI (Brotherhood, 1984; Burke, 1990). Athletes trying to make weight or those with poor nutritional habits may be at risk of not meeting the RDA/RNI for vitamins and minerals (Burke and Read, 1993). These athletes can usually be educated about food choices that will allow them to meet their needs without resorting to supplementation.

Adverse Effects

There appears to be no side effects of vitamin/mineral supplements up to the RDA/RNI. Chronic supplementation in large doses of many vitamins and minerals can lead to a variety of problems (Williams, 1998) particularly vitamins A, D, niacin, and B_6.

Legal Issues

Vitamin/mineral supplements, as long as they do not contain other illegal substances, are not banned substances.

Recommendations

There is no scientific evidence to support the notion that supplementation beyond the RDA/RNI will enhance performance. Those athletes trying to lose weight, strict vegetarians who have limited variety in their diet, and those who consume large quantities of highly processed foods may benefit from a multivitamin/mineral supplement to bring their intake up to the RDA/RNI.

Iron

Iron is an essential part of the oxygen delivery system as part of both haemoglobin and myoglobin (oxygen carriers in the blood and muscle). Low iron levels in athletes are a contributing factor in a disorder called "sports anaemia" (Newhouse and Clement, 1988; Eichner, 1988). Sports anaemia is seen to occur primarily in female endurance athletes although, male endurance athletes are also at risk. Low iron levels, as measured by serum ferritin, may occur through a combination of factors. Growth, menstrual blood loss, sweat, and destruction of red blood cells through training increase the athletes requirement for iron. Haymes and Lamanca (1988) have suggested that the RDA for iron be increased for athletes in heavy training (Table 2). While male athletes seem to be able to meet the increased iron needs through diet many female athlete have difficulty obtaining the existing RDA let alone any increased RDA (Burke and Read, 1993).

The treatment of an iron deficiency is the use of a high dose (100-200 mg) oral supplement for one to three months (Burke and Read, 1993). While supplementation with iron improves iron status in the body the results of iron supplementation on performance are mixed with many studies showing no performance increases following supplementation (Burke and Read, 1993; Williams, 1998; Hultman, Harris, and Spriet, 1999).

Prevention of iron deficiency in at risk athletes is often a more economically viable alternative to regular testing and treatment of a deficiency when it occurs. Haymes and Lamanca (1984) have suggested the use of a low dose supplement of 18mg of elemental iron daily.

Table 2. Iron requirements for Various Populations

Population	RDA (mg)	
	Non Athletes	Athletes
Adult Males	10	17.5
Teenage Males	12	17.5
Females	15	23

Adverse Effects

Supplementation with doses up to the RDA/RNI appears to be safe. Larger doses may cause, gastrointestinal discomfort, toxicity, constipation and in some cases hemochromatosis, the excessive storage of iron in the liver leading to cirrhosis and possible death (Williams, 1998). In addition, iron supplementation can interfere with the absorption of zinc and copper leading to deficiencies in these nutrients (Burke and Read, 1993).

Legal Issues

Iron supplements are not banned substances for athletic competition.

Recommendations

Supplementing with iron does not improve performance unless the athlete is deficient. While some recommendations have been made regarding the use of up to 18 mg of iron per day, the preferred method of increasing iron intake is through increased dietary intake (Hultman, Harris, and Spriet, 1999). Dietary iron can be increased by eating more lean red meat or dark meat of chicken, cooking in cast-iron cookware, eating dried beans or peas with poultry or seafood to improve the absorption of iron from the vegetables, or consume a beverage high in vitamin C when eating bread or cereal. Tea and coffee intake should be avoided when eating foods high in iron. Tea decreases iron absorption by about 60% and coffee decreases it by about 40% (Fairbanks, 1999). If a supplement is taken it should be done under the guidance of a physician.

Other Substances

There are literally hundreds of other supplements on the market that will not be discussed here. In 1994 legislation changes in the U.S. have allowed many substances that were previously available by prescription only to become classified as nutritional/ergogenic supplements. Athletes who are subject to drug testing have to be more careful than ever about what they buy since many over-the-counter supplements will cause positive tests.

Fat Burners/ Weight Loss Supplements

It may be tempting for some lightweight rowers to try these to help them make weight. They are also used by many athletes for an energy boost. While these substances can be effective, they contain ephedrine, ephedra or Mau Huang all of which will result in a positive test for ephedrine which a sympathomimetic drug. This class of drug mimics the effects of adrenaline and stimulates the nervous system.

Ginseng

Ginseng is a plant extract that is supposed to provided a myriad of performance benefits by stimulating the pituitary gland (the master gland and control centre for many of the body's' hormones). Many people who take ginseng preparations report feeling more energetic, and alert. There is no reputable scientific evidence to support the claims of ginseng. Unfortunately, the commercially marketed ginseng preparations contain very little ginseng. In a recent survey of 50 different brands, 88% of them contained less than 9% ginseng. Some of these products contained large amounts of ephedrine, which explains the increased energy and alertness that people report.

Steroid Replacements

There are several substances on the market, notably DHEA which claims to be a steroid replacement. Many of these products are effective for increasing muscle mass and decreasing fat levels. They tend to be most effective in people older than 50 who no longer produce natural DHEA. DHEA, is a corticosteroid that can enhance testosterone production and as such is banned by the IOC.

Conclusion

Nutritional supplements may be effective at improving performance if the athlete is deficient in a nutrient but, there are few if any supplements that will help the performance of a rower. Most are, at best, a waste of money. At worst, they may result in a positive drug test which can ruin a rowers career and reputation as an athlete.

A sound diet that provides adequate energy from a variety of food is more than adequate for the nutritional needs of even the hardest training athlete.

References

Balsom, P., Soderlund, K., and Ekblom, B. (1994). Creatine in humans with special reference to creatine supplementation. Sports Med. 18 (4): 268-280.

Balsom P. et al. (1993). Creatine supplementation and dynamic high intensity intermittent exercise. Scand. J. Med. Sci. Sports. 3: 143-149.

Balsom P. et al. (1993b). Creatine supplementation per se does not enhance endurance exercise performance. Acta Physiol. Scand. 149: 521-523.

Belko, A. (1987). Vitamins and exercise - an update. Med Sci. Sports and Exerc. 19(suppl): 191-196.

Bergstom, J., et al.,(1974). Intracellular free amino acid concentration in human muscle tissue., J Appl. Physiol. 36: 693-697.

Broberg, S., and Sahlin, K. (1989). Adenine nucleotide degradation in human skeletal muscle during prolonged exercise. J. Appl. Physiol. 67: 116-122.

Brotherhood, J. (1984). Nutrition and sport performance. Sports Med. 1: 350-389.

Burke, L. (1990). Dietary intake and food use of groups of elite Australian male athletes. , PhD thesis, Deakin University, Geelong, Australia.

Burke, L., and Read, R. (1993). dietary supplements in sport. Sports Med. 15(1): 43-65.

Castell, L.M. et al.,(1997). Some aspects of the acute phase response after a marathon race, and the effects of glutamine supplementation., Eur. J. Appl. Physiol. 75: 47-53.

Costill, D., Dalsky, G., and Fink, W. (1978). Effects of caffeine ingestion on metabolism and exercise performance. Med. Sci. Sports. Exerc. 10: 155-158.

Damian, A.C. and Pitts, R.F.,(1970). Rates of glutaminase 1 and glutamine synthetase reactions in rat kidney in vivo., Am. J. Physiol. 218: 1249-1255.

Economos, C., Bortz, S., and Nelson, M. (1993). Nutritional practices of elite athletes. Sports Med. 16(6): 381-399.

Eichner, E. (1988). 'Sports Anaemia': poor terminology for a real phenomenon. Gatorade Sport Science Exchange. 1(6).

Fairbanks, V. (1999). Iron in medicine and nutrition. in Modern Nutrition in Health and Disease (Shils, Olson, Shike, and Ross. eds.) William & Wilkins. Baltimore,Maryland.

Friedl, K. (1992). Ergogenic aids: clenbuterol. Ma Huang, caffeine, L-carnitine, and growth hormone releasers. NSCA Journal. 14(4): 35-44.

Goldstein, L., and Schrock, H.,(1980) Relationship of muscle gluta-mine production to renal ammonia metabolism. Biochem. Soc. Trans. 8: 509-510.

Graham, T., Rush, J., and van Soeren, M. (1994). Caffeine and exer-cise: metabolism and performance. Can. J. Appl. Physiol. 19(1): 111-138.

Greenhaff, P. et al. (1993). Influence of oral creatine supplementa-tion n muscle torque during repeated bouts of maximal voluntary exercise in man. Clin. Sci. 84: 565-571.

Harris, R., Soderlund, K., and Hultman, E. (1992). Elevation of cre-atine in resting and exercise muscles of normal subjects by creatine supplementation. Clin. Sci. 83: 367-374.

Haymes, E., and Lamanca, L. (1989)Iron loss in runners during exercise: implications and recommendations. Sport Med. 7: 277-285.

Hoogwerf, B., Laine, D., and Greene, E. (1986). Urine C-peptide and creatine (Jaffe method) excretion in healthy young adults on varied diets: sustained effects of carbohydrate, protein, and meat content. Am. J. Clin. Nutr. 43: 350-360.

Hultman, E., Harris, R., and Spriet, L. (1999). Diet in work and exercise performance. in Modern Nutrition in Health and Disease (Shils, Olson, Shike, and Ross. eds.) William & Wilkins.

Baltimore,Maryland.

Keast, D., et al., (1995). Depression of plasma glutamine following exercise stress and its possible influence on the immune system.", Med J Aus 162: 15-18.

Kirskey, B et al. (1999). The effects of 6 weeks of creatine monohydrate supplementation on performance measures and body composition in collegiate track and field athletes. J. Strength Cond. Res. 13(2): 148-156.

Kreider, R. (1995). The effect of creatine loading on muscular strength and body composition. Strength and Conditioning. 17(5): 72-73.

Lefavi, R. et al. (1998). Effects of creatine monohydrate on performance of college baseball and basketball players. J. Strength Cond. Res. 12(4): 275.

Linderman, J., and Gosselink, K., (1994).The effects of sodium bicarbonate ingestion on exercise performance. Sports Medicine. 18(2) 75-80.

Maclennan, P.A., et al. A positive relationship between protein synthesis rate and intracellular glutamine concentration in perfused rat skeletal muscle. FEBS Lett 215:187-191.

Max, Stephen.,(1990). Glucocorticoid-mediated induction of glutamine synthetase in skeletal muscle.", Med. Sci. Sports Exerc. 22 (3): 325-330.

Newhouse, I., and Clement, D.(1988). Iron Status in athletes: an update. Sport Medicine. 5: 337-352.

Newsholme, E.A., and Parry Billings, M., (1990). Properties of glutamine release from muscle and its importance for the immune system. J. Parenter. Enter. Nutr. 14: 635-675.

Peeters, B., Lantz, C., and Mayhew, J. (1999). Effects of oral creatine monohydrate and creatine phosphate supplementation on maximal strength indices, body composition, and blood pressure. J. Strength Cond. Res. 13(1): 3-9.

Pitts, R.F., et al.,(1972). Metabolism of glutamine by the intact functioning kidney of the dog. J. Clin. Invest. 51:557-565.

Plisk, S., and Kreider, R. (1999). Creatine controversy? Strength and Conditioning Journal. 21(1):14-23.

Rossiter, H., Cannell, E., and Jakeman, P., (1996). The effect of oral creatine supplementation on the 1000-m performance of competitive rowers. Journal of Sport Sciences. 14: 175-179

Rowbottom, David et al.,(1996). The Emerging Role of Glutamine as an Indicator of Exercise Stress and Overtraining. Sports Med. 21 (2): 80-97.

Rowbottom et al., (1995). The haematological, biochemical and immunological profile of athletes suffering from the overtraining syndrome. Eur. J. Apll. Physiol. 70: 502-509.

Shewchuk, Leann et al., (1997). Dietary L-glutamine does not improve lymphocyte metabolism or function in exercised-trained rats. Med. Sci. Sports Exerc. 29 (4): 474-481.

Soderlund, K., Greenhaff, P., and Hultman, E. (1992). Energy metabolism in type I and Type II human muscle fibres during short term electrical stimulation at different frequencies. Acta Physiol. Scand. 144: 15-22

Soderlund, K., Balsom, P., and Ekblom, B. (1994). Creatine supplementation and high intensity exercise: influence on performance and muscle metabolism. Clin. Sci. 87 suppl.: 120

Souba, W.W., (1992). Glutamine: physiology, biochemistry and nutrition in critical illness. R.G. Landers: Austin Texas.

Tarnopolsky, M. (1994). Caffeine and endurance performance. Sports Med. 18(2): 109-125.

Tesch, P., Thorsson, A., and Fujitsuka, N. (1989). Creatine phosphate in fibre types of skeletal muscle before and after exhaustive exercise. J. Appl. Physiol. 66: 1756-1759.

Walker, J. (1960). Creatine: biosynthesis, regulation and function. In: Mister, A., editor. Advances in enzymology and related areas of molecular biology. New York: John Wiley.

Williams, M. (1995) Nutritional ergogenics in athletics. Journal of Sport Sciences. 13(S63-S74)

Williams, M. (1998) The Ergogenics Edge. Human Kinetics Publishers. Champaign Ill.

Weight Loss and Making Weight

11

Lightweight rowers are often faced with the challenge of decreasing bodyweight. Failure to be under the required weight (160 lbs for men and 130 lbs for women) results in disqualification of the individual or crew. While weight loss is of greatest importance to lightweight rowers heavyweights also tend to lose some weight as they approach the competitive season (Secher, 1993). In some cases heavyweights decrease bodyweight due to the increased training volume. For others weight, and specifically fat mass, is decreased as a means of improving relative strength and aerobic power (Fogelholm, 1994).

Weight loss can either be done gradually (more than days) or rapidly (less than days). Rapid bodyweight losses are normally accomplished through dehydration while gradual weight loss is normally accomplished through a negative energy balance.

Rapid Weight Loss

Rapid weight loss is usually done over a period of hours. Wrestlers have been known to decrease weight by 4.5 to 4.9% in a 12- to 24-hour period (Zambraski et al, 1976; Webster, Rutt, and Weltman, 1985). Rapid weight loss is usually brought about through the use of rubber suits while exercising, fluid restriction, food restriction, and saunas (Fogelholm, 1994). Viitasalo et al. (1987) found that weight could be reduced by 2 to 5% in less than 2.5 hours using a sauna set at 80 to 85° C. Some athletes resort to the use of laxatives or dieuretics when making weight. While they do decrease weight, these substances often result in gastrointestinal upset, and the use of dieuretics will result in a positive drug test in amateur competitions.

Effects on Performance

Weight Regain

The amount of weight the athlete regains following the weigh-in is variable but is related to the time between weigh-in and the competition. Klingzing and Karpowicz (1987) found that 21% of the weight lost could be regained within one hour. Other studies have shown regain of 42 to 100% of weight lost in three to five hours (Fogelholm, 1994). Since rowing weigh-ins are normally done one to two hours prior to the race, rowers can expect to regain 20 to 30% of the weight they lost.

Aerobic Power

Time to exhaustion is decreased following dehydration (Fogelholm, 1994). Weight loss following a short dietary restriction resulted in a decrease in aerobic capacity of 10% (Webster, Rutt, and Weltman, 1985). The magnitude and speed of weight loss can have an effect on aerobic power. VO_2 max was decreased with a weight loss of 4.9% in 12 to 24 hours but was maintained with weight loss of 1.6 to 3.4% in two to 48 hours (Fogelholm, 1994).

Anaerobic Power

Rowing is predominately an aerobic sport, but the anaerobic system contributes about 20% of the energy production and is the main energy system used at the start and during the final sprint. Decreased anaerobic performance has been seen in most studies that looked at dehydration and performance (Hickner et al., 1991; Horswill et al., 1990). A short rehydration period (1 to 3 hours) does not return anaerobic performance to normal levels. However, if five or more hours are available for rehydration between weigh-in and race time there is no effect on anaerobic performance.

Strength

Strength like anaerobic power is decreased as a result of dehydration. Strength levels do not appear to return to normal unless five or more hours are available for rehydration.

Causes of Decreased Performance

The dietary restrictions during rapid weight loss often involve either a complete fast or the elimination of carbohydrate from the diet. This is done because the depletion of the body's carbohydrate stores results in rapid water losses (one gram of carbohydrate binds to three to four grams of water in the body). The intensity of a rowing race is high enough that the only source of energy to a rower is carbohydrate. When depleted, both speed and technical abilities will be decreased. Horswill et al. (1990) found that a diet high in carbohydrate helped maintain performance following rapid weight loss. A high-protein, low-carbohydrate diet during rapid weight loss also affects the body's buffering system (Greenhaff et al., 1987). This means that the lactic acid produced during racing cannot be efficiently dealt with and will cause greater fatigue sooner.

When dehydrated, plasma volume, stroke volume, and cardiac output are all decreased (Fogelholm, 1994). Oxygen transport to the muscles, nutrient exchange, waste removal, and heat dissipation are all impaired.

Psychologically rapid weight reduction can alter mood, increase feelings of fatigue, anxiety, and anger. Constant thirst and the inability to cool the body can make the athlete feel weak, dizzy and decrease mental functioning. If a large percentage of bodyweight is lost through dehydration serious health problems can occur (table 1).

Table 1. Effects of various degrees of dehydration on performance and health

% Weight Lost	Physiological Effect
1	Thirst
2-3	Stronger thirst. loss of appetite, vague discomfort Hemoconcentration
4-5	Economy of movement Lagging pace, flushed skin, apathy, nausea, impatience, emotional instability
6-7	Headache, stumbling, heat exhaustion, increased body temperature, pulse rate, and respiration
7-9	Laboured breathing, dizziness, indistinct speech, increased weakness and mental confusion
10-13	Spastic muscles, general incapacity, delirium, decreased blood volume, decreased renal function, swollen tongue, circulatory insufficiency
14-20	Shrivelled skin, inability to swallow, dim vision, painful urination, cessation of urine formation, deafness, numb skin
20+	Death

Gradual Weight Loss

There has been very little research on the effects of gradual weight loss on the performance of competitive athletes. While there are many studies using untrained individuals it is difficult to apply this data to athletes since the athletes tend to have much less body fat that they can lose.

In high-level athletes, diet is the only way to achieve the energy imbalance needed to decrease bodyweight. This is because the work volume of elite rowers is so high it cannot be raised any further. Lower level rowers could use dietary manipulation or maintain their current food intake and increase their volume of training.

A gradual weight loss is normally accomplished by reducing the fat intake in the diet while maintaining carbohydrate and protein levels. This approach seems to help maintain performance. Aerobic, anaerobic, and strength performances may even increase as a result of the lower bodyweight (Fogelholm, 1994). Costill et al. (1988) found that swimmers, who have similar training patterns to rowers, could not maintain their training volumes when carbohydrate intake was reduced below 5.3 g/kg of bodyweight. They were able to maintain training volume when consuming 8.2 g/kg. It has been suggested that a carbohydrate intake of 10 g/kg may be needed to replenish carbohydrate stores within a 24-hour period (Robergs, 1991).

The normal recommendation for protein intake is 0.8g/kg. During periods of weight loss this does not appear to be enough to maintain muscle mass. A slight increase in protein to 1.0 to 1.6 g/kg seems to be necessary (Fogelholm, 1994). This is the amount of protein that endurance athletes typically consume when not trying to lose weight (Economos, Bortz, and Nelson, 1993), so there is no need for most athletes to adjust their protein intake when dieting. Strict vegetarians may be the exception in that they often have difficulty obtaining all the protein they need.

In order to decrease bodyweight, the athlete must achieve an energy imbalance. This means they must consume fewer calories than they use. Ideally, weight loss should be primarily fat loss. There are about 9000 Kcal/kg of fat. Recommendations for the general population have been that weight loss should not exceed 0.5 kg/week if muscle mass is to be maintained. This recommendation may not apply to athletes. Yarrows (1988) has suggested athletes can lose one to 1.5 kg/week and still maintain muscle mass. A weight loss of 1 kg/week would mean the athlete would have to consume ≈ 1300 Kcal/day less than they expend.

Economos, Bortz, and Nelson (1993) have recommended that male athletes who train more than 90 minutes per day consume 50 to 60 Kcal/kg of bodyweight each day and female athletes should consume 45 to 50 Kcal/kg. In order to lose 1 kg/week a lightweight male rower would need to decrease their energy intake to 32 to 42 Kcal/kg/day. A lightweight female rower would have to decrease her intake to 21 to 26 Kcal/kg/day.

Accepting the following:

1 g carbohydrate = 4 kcal
1 g protein = 4 kcal
1 g fat = 9 kcal

and knowing that a rower needs:

7-10 g/kg of carbohydrate
1.0-1.6 g/kg of protein

We can calculate that lightweight rowers can maintain muscle mass and have adequate carbohydrate for training if they consumed > 32 kcal/kg/day. Therefore, a lightweight male who eats 42 kcal/kg/day should be able to lose 1 kg/week and still be able to train adequately. Since our calculations are expressed per unit of bodyweight both males and females have the same minimum requirements (32kcal/kg/day). Since a female would have to consume 21 to 26 kcal/kg/day to lose 1 kg per week and this is less than the minimum they require, lightweight women should consider losing no more than 0.5 to 0.75 kg/week.

These numbers and calculations are based on averages and will vary slightly from athlete to athlete. They can be affected by lean body mass, age, and fitness level. They do, however, offer a good starting point from which to make recommendations based on average light-weights. Accurate measures of calorie expenditure can be made using the same procedures discussed in the direct measures section of the chapter on determining training zones. If this is accompanied by diet log records, individual recommendations for weight loss can be calculated.

Coaches need to be aware of the techniques and frequency with which their athletes are trying to make weight. There has been concern expressed by researchers that frequent weight loss may lead to the development of anorexia nervosa or bulimia (Fogelholm, 1994). This seems to occur most often in female athletes who have a preoccupation with physical appearance. It seems to occur less frequently if the athlete is more focused on performance than appearance.

Recommendations

Weight loss is a serious issue for athletes. Prior to starting a weight loss program a meeting between the coach, athlete, physician, and a dietician should occur. One of the first things that will be decided by the group is if it is in the athletes best interest, both short and long term, to try to make weight. Often high school- and college-aged athletes are 3 to 4 kg over the lightweight cut off but manage to make the weight at competition time. Athletes who are still growing need to consider whether or not they should make an effort to increase their weight through strength training. They will probably become heavyweights by the time they have stopped growing, and fighting to make the lightweight cut off may negatively impact on their long term development as a heavyweight rower.

The amount of weight that needs to be lost and off season body composition of the athlete affect the type of weight loss. Small amounts of weight (1 to 3% of bodyweight) can be achieved through one to two days of rapid weight loss without significant impact on performance. Larger weight loss should be accomplished through a combination of gradual and rapid weight loss. Total weight loss should be limited to 5 to 7% of bodyweight (4 to 6 kg for men and 3 to 5 kg for women) unless the athlete has a high initial level of body fat. If the athlete needs to lose more than this they should consider rowing heavyweight.

References

Costill, D. et al. (1988). Effects of repeated days of intensified training on muscle glycogen and swimming performance. Med. Sci. Sports Exerc. 20: 249-254.

Economos, C., Bortz, S., and Nelson, M. (1993). Nutritional practices of elite athletes: practical recommendations. Sports Med. 16: 381-399.

Fogelholm, M. (1994). Effects of bodyweight reduction on sports performance. Sports Med. 18: 249-267.

Greenhaff, P. et al. (1987). Dietary composition and acid-base status: limiting factors in the performance of maximal exercise in man? Eur. J. Appl. Physiol. 56: 444-450.

Hickner, R., et al. (1991). Test development for the study of physical performance in wrestlers following weight loss. Int. J. Sports Med. 12: 557-562.

Horswill, C. et al. (1990). Weight loss, dietary carbohydrate modifications, and high intensity, physical performance. Med. Sci. Sports Exerc. 22: 470-476.

Klinzing, J., and Karpowicz, W. (1986). The effect of a rapid weight loss and rehydration on a wrestling performance. J. Sports Med. Phys. Fitness. 26: 149-156.

Robergs, R. (1991). Nutrition and exercise determinants of postexercise glycogen synthesis. Int. J. Sports Nutr. 1: 307-337.

Secher, N. (1993). Physiological and biomechanical aspects of rowing: implications for training. Sports Med. 15: 24-42.

Viitasalo, J., et al. (1987). effects of rapid weight reduction on force production and vertical jumping height. Int. J. Sports Med. 8: 281-285.

Wardlaw, G. (1997). Contemporary Nutrition. WCB McGraw Hill publishers. NY: NY.

Webster, S., Rutt, R. , and Weltman, A. (1990). Physiological effects of a weight loss regimen practiced by college wrestlers. Med. Sci. Sports Exerc. 22: 229-234.

Yarrows, S. (1988). Weight loss through dehydration in amateur wrestling. J. Am. Diet Assoc. 88: 491-493.

Zambraski, E. et al. (1976). Iowa wrestling study: weight loss and urinary profiles of collegiate wrestlers. Med. Sci. Sports Exerc. 8: 105-108.

Energy Demands and Nutritional Requirements of Rowing

12

A muscle needs a constant supply of energy in order to contract. Higher levels of work require more energy. Rowers are capable of expending huge amounts of energy during training and racing. If their energy stores become depleted the ability to train, recover, and compete is impaired. An understanding of the energy processes of the body makes it possible to determine how much and what an athlete needs to eat to maximize performance.

Energy Systems

The human body uses ATP (adenosinetriphosphate) as its energy source. While it is common for coaches and athletes to talk in terms of carbohydrate, fat, and protein as energy sources, these macronutients and must be converted to ATP before they can be used.

There are three systems through which ATP is produced: The anaerobic alactic system, anaerobic glycolysis, and the aerobic system (which consists of the beta oxidation, the Krebs cycle, and electron transport chain). These energy systems are chains of chemical reactions that convert potential food energy into useable ATP. Figure 1 shows the pathways that the different substrates take.

Anaerobic Alactic System

The anaerobic alactic system is the first energy system used during any sort of activity. It is made up of ATP stored in the muscle and CP (creatine phosphate). This energy system is used for the first few seconds of exercise and allows the body to achieve very high power outputs. This energy system is the primary contributor to activities lasting up to 15s (Margaria, 1964). The capacity of this system is a function of the rate of energy use (power output). In a 100m sprint this system lasts for about six seconds. In rowing, the recovery portion of each stroke allows this system to partially recharge increas-

Figure 1. Substrate pathways. Each arrow represents a series of chemical reactions.

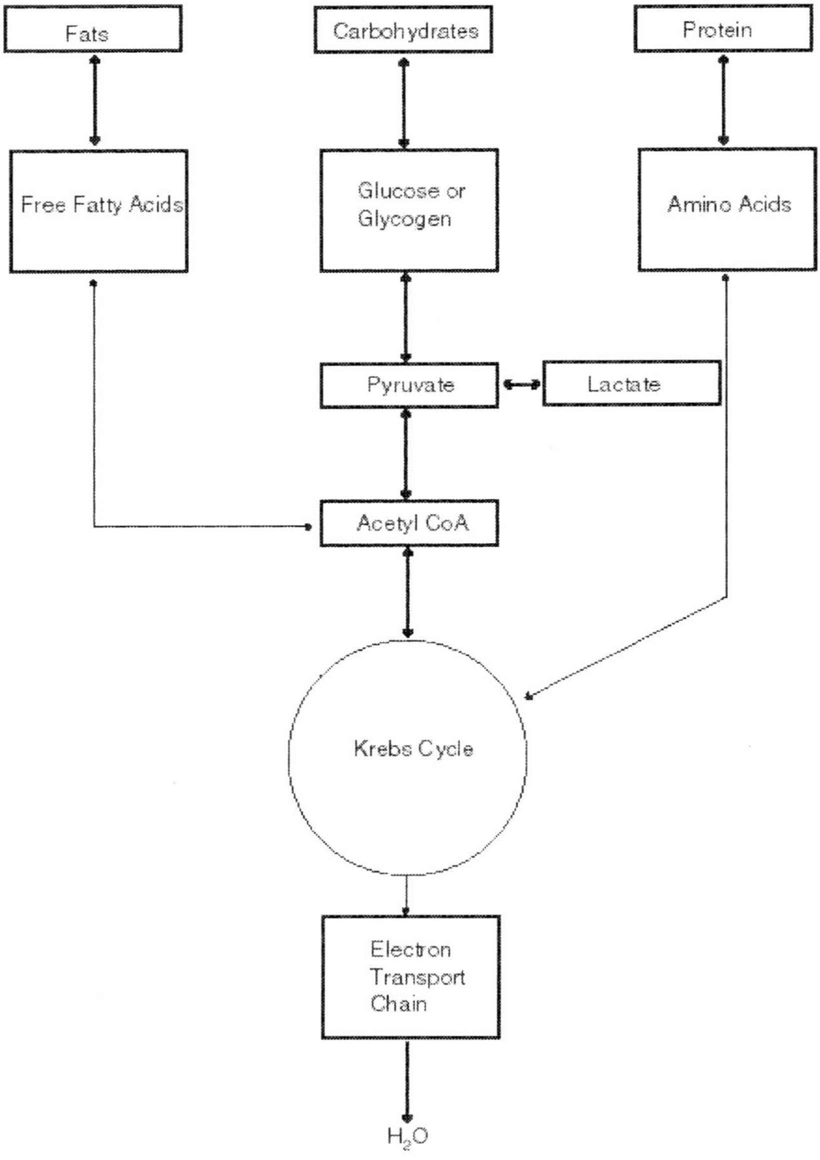

ing the capacity of the system to 15s or slightly more.

Anaerobic Glycolysis

Anaerobic glycolysis converts carbohydrate, in the form of glycogen, to energy and pyruvic acid. Pyruvic acid is then either converted to lactic acid or acetyl co-A, which is used in the aerobic system. The accumulation of lactic acid as a result of using this system can lead to fatigue, and decreased performance. This energy system cannot produce energy at as high a rate as the anaerobic alactic system and is activated as the alactic system starts to become depleted.

Aerobic System

The aerobic system is the last system activated. It has the lowest rate of energy production but is capable of producing energy for hours rather than seconds or minutes like the other systems. The aerobic system can convert protein, carbohydrate, and fat to ATP.

Integration of Energy Systems

While it is convenient to think of the energy systems as single entities that work independently of each other, the fact is they are an integrated system. The energy systems work together in an attempt to maintain the desired work level. As one system becomes depleted another starts up to maintain energy production (Green, 1991). Figure 2 shows the relationship between the three energy systems.

Energy Systems and Muscle Fibre Types

Muscle fibres, in humans, can be divided into two broad categories, a summary of the fibre types can be seen in Table 1. Slow twitch (ST), also known as type I fibres, are capable of working for extended periods of time. This is due, in part, to their metabolic profile which favours energy production through aerobic pathways

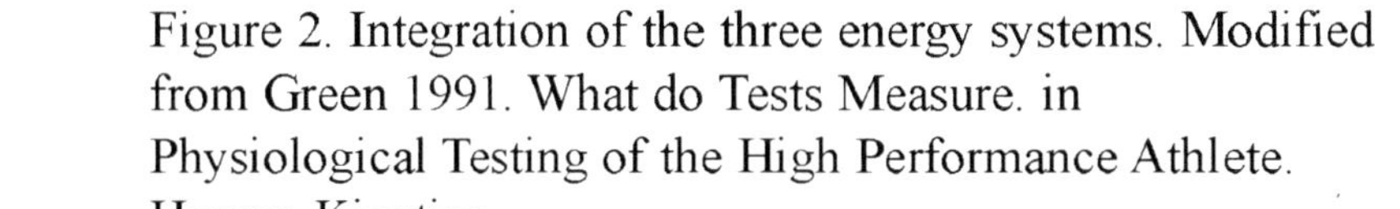

Figure 2. Integration of the three energy systems. Modified from Green 1991. What do Tests Measure. in Physiological Testing of the High Performance Athlete. Human Kinetics.

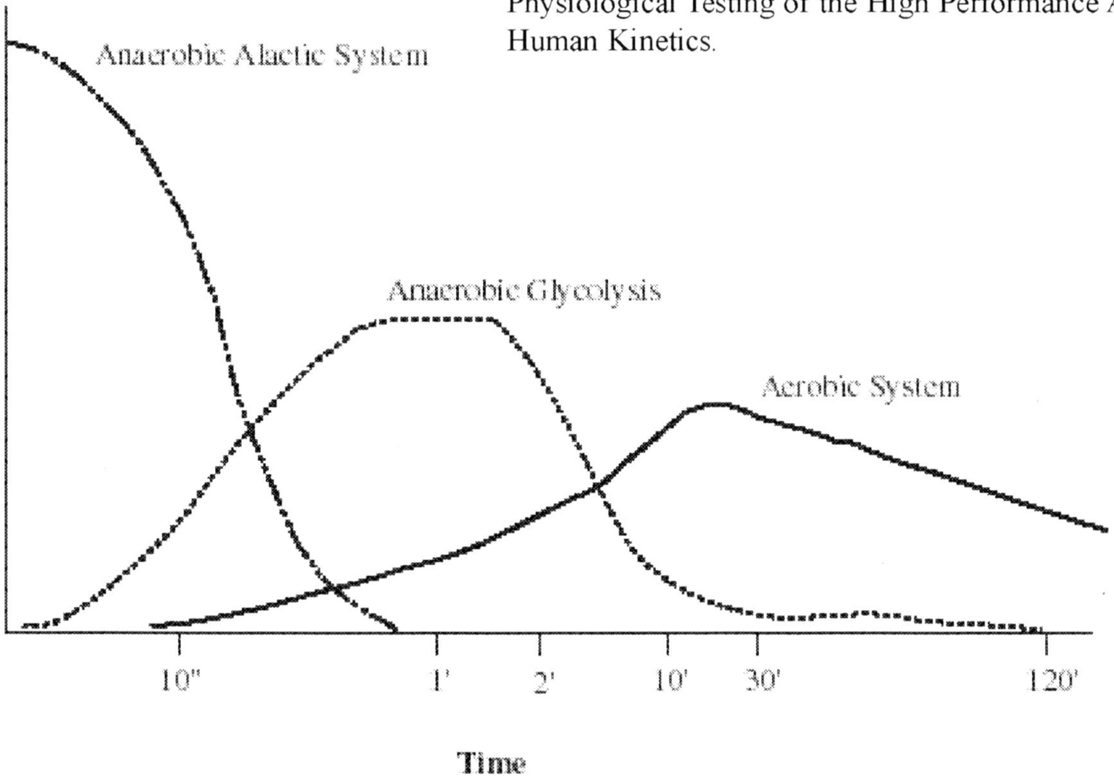

Table 1. Characteristics of Four Fibre Types

	ST (slow twitch)	**FOG** (fast oxidative glycolytic)	**FTc** (undifferentiated)	**FT** (Fast Glycolytic)
Aerobic Capacity	Very High	High	Moderate	Low
Anaerobic Alactic	Low	Moderate	High	Very High
Anaerobic Glycol.	Low	Moderate	High	Very High
Peak Power	Low	Moderate	High	Very High
Time to Fatigue	Very High	High	Moderate	Low
Preferred Fuel	CHO, Fat	CHO	CHO	CHO

(Salmons, 1994). Fast twitch fibres can be subdivided into three categories. Fast twitch glycolytic (FT), type IIb, fibres produce energy predominantly through anaerobic pathways and are capable of high power production, but only for short periods of time (Salmons, 1994). Fast twitch oxidative-glycolytic (FOG), type IIa, are not as adept at power production as the FT fibres, but they produce more power than the ST fibres. The FOG fibres are capable of generating energy through both aerobic and anaerobic pathways, this makes them an endurance fibre of intermediate power production (Salomons, 1994). The final type of fast twitch fibre is the undifferentiated fast twitch (FTc) or type IIc fibre. The functions and metabolic capacities of this fibre are, at present, not completely understood. However, it is believed these fibres are in the process of becoming either FOG or FT fibres (Larsson and Forsberg, 1980).

Table 2. Percentages of calories coming from fat and CHO during a 60 minute training session in each of the categories

Category	% Fat	% CHO
VI	65	35
V	30	70
IV	10	90
III	0	100
II	0	100

The type of fibre used during training is determined by the training category used (see training categories chapter). Since the different muscle fibre types have different capacities to use the various energy systems the training category used also affects the source of energy.

Table 2 shows the relationship between the training categories and the proportions of fat and carbohydrate that are used. Protein is not included in the table because most protein is converted to carbohydrate before it is used and is therefore reflected in the carbohydrate use.

The use of fat as a primary fuel in CAT VI is one of the reasons that this category is so important. The body's carbohydrate stores are limited. Once they become depleted the athlete can no longer perform at higher work intensities (Hermansen, Hultman, and Saltin, 1967). Training in category VI, which relies predominately on fat, can increase the total work volume before fatigue. This allows the athlete to improve both physiological and technically.

Energy Requirements of Rowing

General recommendations for energy intake for athletes have been published (Economos, Bortz, and Nelson, 1993). Male athletes, training more than 90 minutes per day, should consume in excess of 50 kcal/kg of body weight. Female athletes training for similar time periods should consume 45 to 50 kcal/kg of bodyweight.

These averages are suitable as a starting point. However, if athletes are having trouble maintaining body weight or there appears to be a lack of progress in training, they should have both energy intake and expenditure measured.

Energy intake can be measured using various dietary recall methods and nutritional software. The amount and type of energy that is used can be determined by measuring the amount of oxygen and carbon dioxide that is consumed and produced at rest or during exercise. It is known that for every litre of oxygen consumed approximately 5 kcal are released. The respiratory exchange ratio (the ratio of CO_2/O_2) is an indicator of how much fat and carbohydrate are being used. It is this sort of information that will be used in the calculations of the energy requirements for rowing.

Sample Calculations

The calculations below are estimates of the energy required for a training session, and the daily energy requirements for a rower. These are estimates and can vary from athlete to athlete. The purpose of these calculations is to make you think about the amount of food that needs to be consumed by competitive rowers.

Background

Before starting the calculation the athlete must be tested to have their thresholds and VO_2 max determined. The information below is derived from such a test.

- The athlete is an adult male heavy weight athlete
- The athlete is competitive but not at an international level
- The athlete is a small heavy weight (185 lb. 84 kg)
- The athlete has a VO_2 max. of 5 L/min.
- The Athlete has an anaerobic threshold (category IV) at 85% of VO_2 max. and an aerobic threshold (category VI) at 70% VO_2 max.

Energy cost of a training session

Using these numbers we can estimate the energy demand for a category VI and a category IV training session for this athlete.

Category VI (120 minutes)

We know that this athlete has a category VI that is 70% of VO_2 max. This means that 3.5 L/min. of oxygen will be consumed during this training session. Since 1L of oxygen releases 5 kcal this athlete will use 17.5 kcal/ min. during this session. During the 120 minutes a total of 2100 kcal will be burned.

Category IV (90 minutes)

We know that this athlete has a category IV that is 85% of VO2 max. This means that 4.25 L/min. of oxygen will be consumed during this training session. Since 1L of oxygen releases 5 kcal this athlete will use 21.25 kcal/ min. during this session. During the 90 minutes a total of 1912 kcal will be burned.

Daily Energy Requirements

The amount of energy required each day is the sum of the energy required for normal body function, miscellaneous activity, and training.

Energy Needed for Normal Body Function	3000
Energy for Training Session 1 (Cat. VI)	2100
Energy for Training Session 2 (Cat IV)	1912
Miscellaneous activity	500
Total	**7512**

An athlete such as the one discussed here needs to consume more than 7500 calories per day to maintain body weight and replenish energy stores. If we had used the general recommendation of 50 kcal/kg this athlete would have been consuming about 4200 kcal/day, much less than they actually need. This shows the importance of actually measuring the energy requirements of the athlete, if possible.

While some people may think it is great to be able to consume 7500 or more calories per day many athletes find it difficult to eat this often. The carbohydrates needed to fuel the exercise are very filling causing some athletes to constantly feel "stuffed," making it difficult to train. On the other hand, if the athlete does not consume enough energy they will become chronically carbohydrate depleted and overtrained.

Energy and Food

There are three macronutrients responsible for providing energy. These are protein, fat and carbohydrate. While vitamins, minerals and water all play a role in the production of energy they cannot be converted to ATP.

Protein

Protein plays a minimal role as a fuel source during exercise. Only 5 to 10% of the total energy turnover can be attributed to protein (Hultman, Harris, and Spriet, 1999). This may rise to as high as 25% of total during prolonged training sessions or periods of carbohydrate depletion.

The reliance on protein as an energy source can have several negative side effects for the competitive athlete. Glutamine and alanine are two of the amino acids readily converted to energy (Hultman, Harris, and Spriet, 1999). Glutamine is also an important fuel for white blood cells, so reductions in blood glutamine concentration following intense exercise may contribute to immune suppression in overtrained athletes (Parry-Billings et al., 1990a; Parry-Billings et al., 1990b; Parry-Billings et al., 1992; Kargotich et al., 1996; Newsholme and Calder, 1997).

Another group of amino acids that are used for energy are the Branched chain amino acids (BCAA). The availability of BCAA during exercise has been theorized to contribute to fatigue

(Newsholme et al., 1991). During endurance exercise, BCAAs are taken up by the muscles rather than the liver in order to contribute to energy production. The source of BCAAs for energy metabolism during exercise is the plasma BCAA pool, which is replenished through the catabolism of whole body proteins during endurance exercise (Davis, 1995; Kreider, 1998; Newsholme et al., 1991). However, the oxidation of BCAAs in the muscle during prolonged exercise may be greater than capacity to provide BCAAs. This means that the plasma BCAA concentration may decline during prolonged endurance exercise (Blomstrand et al., 1988; Blomstrand et al., 1991). The decline in plasma BCAAs during endurance exercise can result in an increase in the ratio of free tryptophan to BCAAs.

Free tryptophan and BCAAs compete for entry into the brain via the same amino-acid carrier (Newsholme et al., 1991). Therefore, a decrease in BCAAs in the blood allows entry of tryptophan into the brain. The decrease in plasma BCAAs and increase in free tryptophan during prolonged endurance exercise alters the ratio of free tryptophan to BCAAs and increases the entry of tryptophan into the brain (Newsholme et al., 1991). An increased concentration of tryptophan in the brain promotes the formation of the neurotransmitter 5-hydroxytryptamine (5-HT). 5-HT has been shown to induce sleep, depress motor neuron excitability, influence endocrine function, and suppress appetite. An exercise-induced imbalance in the ratio of free tryptophan to BCAAs has been implicated as a possible cause of acute fatigue (central fatigue). It has also been hypothesized that chronic elevations in 5-HT concentration, which may occur in athletes maintaining high-volume training, explains some of the reported signs and symptoms of the overtraining syndrome: postural hypotension, anemia, amenorrhea, immunosuppression, appetite suppression, weight loss, depression, and decreased performance (Newsholme et al., 1991; Gastmann and Lehmann, 1998; Kreider, 1998).

The use of whole body proteins to supply energy will tend to decrease muscle mass. Decreases in muscle mass will ultimately lead to decreased strength and power production thereby decreasing rowing performance. It may seem that since the use of protein can result in many negative side effects that athletes should focus their diets on protein consumption. This is a belief put forth in popular magazines and fitness books yet it has little scientific basis.

Protein Requirements

About 10-15% of total energy intake should come from protein (Hultman, Harris, and Spriet, 1999). For the average individual the RDA/RNI for protein is 0.8g/kg of bodyweight. For endurance athletes, like rowers, 1.2-1.6 g/kg is sufficient (Economos, Bortz, and Nelson, 1993). As long as the energy requirements are met there is little risk of a protein deficiency. In fact, most athletes consume close to 2 g/kg of protein per day (American Dietetic Association, 1987). While many athletes believe in increasing their protein intake through various protein powders or drinks, there is no evidence that high-protein diets (2 or more g/kg/day) will help increase strength or muscle mass (Lemon and Proctor, 1991).

Fats

Fats play a minimal role as an energy source during a rowing race. However, during Cat. VI training fat can be the major fuel source. The use of fat as a primary fuel is one of the reasons that category VI training is so important to rowers. Since there is no risk of running out of fat as a fuel large volumes of training and technical work can be done without the risk of energy depletion.

One of the early adaptations to aerobic training is to increase the storage and ability to use intramuscular fat (Hurley et al. 1986). This increases endurance capacity by decreasing the reliance on carbohydrate as a fuel source.

Daily fat intake for athletes should be between 25% and 30% of total calorie intake (Hultman, Harris, and Spriet, 1999). If an athlete is attempting to decrease body weight fat intake can be lowered to create an energy deficit.

Carbohydrate

Carbohydrates (CHO) are needed to replenish muscle and liver glycogen stores. CHO serve as the primary fuel source during racing and training above cat. VI. In training sessions 60 minutes or longer, CHO depletion is the primary cause of fatigue (Costill, 1988). The depletion of carbohydrates results in a greater reliance on protein and fat as energy sources. The negative side effects of protein metabolism have already been outlined.

Carbohydrate Requirements

It is recommended athletes consume 6 to 10 g of CHO per kilogram of bodyweight. This should account for 55 to 60% of total energy intake (Economos, Bortz, and Nelson, 1993). During periods of heavy training Sherman (1983), has suggested that athletes consume a minimum of 500g of CHO per day or 70% of total energy intake.

Since CHO foods are not energy dense (low calories per gram of food) many athletes report constantly feeling "stuffed" all day long when trying to consume adequate CHO. With some athletes this can affect their ability to train. At higher levels of competition, when rowers may be training three to four times per day, it is often difficult to find the time to eat enough. In both of these situations athletes should be encouraged to consume a high CHO liquid supplement (20 to 25% CHO concentration) to help meet their CHO and energy requirements (Economos, Bortz, and Nelson, 1993).

Type of Carbohydrates

Carbohydrates are most commonly classified as simple or complex Biochemically, most carbohydrate foods can be classified as mono-, di-, or polysaccharides. Simple carbohydrates are the mono and disaccharides. Examples of monosaccharides are fructose, glucose, or galactose. When two of these monosaccharides are linked together with a chemical bond, a disaccharide is produced. Sucrose is made up of one glucose attached to one fructose molecule. Lactose, found in dairy products, is produced by combining a glucose with a galactose molecule. Polysaccharides can be made up of hundreds or thousands of monosaccharides. The starches found in plant foods are polysaccharides made up of many glucose molecules. The two forms of starch are amylose, a straight chain of repeating glucose molecules, and amylopectin, a branched chain. Through digestion or with food processing, starches can be partially broken down to smaller chains, called dextrins and ultimately to their mono or disaccharides.

The Glycaemic Index

The glycaemic index is a method for comparing the blood glucose response of carbohydrate based foods. It was developed to aid individuals with diabetes in controlling their blood sugar levels while consuming a low fat, higher carbohydrate diet (Walton and Rhodes, 1997; Jenkins et al. 1981; Jenkins et al, 1984; Jenkins et al., 1986; Jenkins et al. 1994; Wolever et al., 1991). The glycaemic index is a percentage value of the area under the blood glucose response curve of a food containing 50 g of carbohydrate, divided by the area of the blood glucose response of 50 g of carbohydrate in a reference food, multiplied by 100 (Walton and Rhodes, 1997; Jenkins et al., 1984).

glycaemic index of test food   x 100 /blood glucose area of reference food

The reference food used for calculating the glycaemic index was originally glucose. The glycaemic index of selected foods based on the glucose reference are presented at the end of this chapter. Now white bread containing 50 g of carbohydrate is commonly used instead of glucose. Bread is preferred to glucose because it is more palatable and avoids the possibility of delayed gastric emptying from the high osmolality of a glucose solution (Jenkins et al., 1984). The use of a standard food for comparison makes the glycaemic index a more powerful tool than the glycaemic response of individual foods. The use of a standard removes most of the error associated with individual differences in digestion and absorption rates (Wolever, 1992).

The development of the glycaemic index demonstrated that carbohydrate structure could not be used as the sole predictor of physiological responses (Jenkins et al. 1981). This became obvious when Jenkins et al.(1981) found the glycaemic index of sucrose to be 59, compared with 80 for potatoes and 72 for rice.

With the glycaemic index foods can be categorised according to into, a low, moderate, or high glycaemic index groups. Low glycaemic foods cause the least glycaemic response and high glycaemic foods elicit a comparably greater glycaemic response. Figure 3 shows the glycaemic responses of high, low and moderate glycaemic index foods. Also of importance is that the high glycaemic index foods cause a greater insulin response than low or moderate glycaemic foods.

Unfortunately, the glycaemic index has been criticised because it only gives a value for a single food and not meals (Walton and Rhodes, 1997). In a 1986 study, Wolever and Jenkins found the glycaemic index for individual foods could be used to predict the glycaemic index for a meal. The glycaemic index calculation for the meal was strongly correlated with the area under the glucose response curve for meals containing fat and protein.
Hollenbeck and Coulston (1991) argue the glycaemic index is inef-

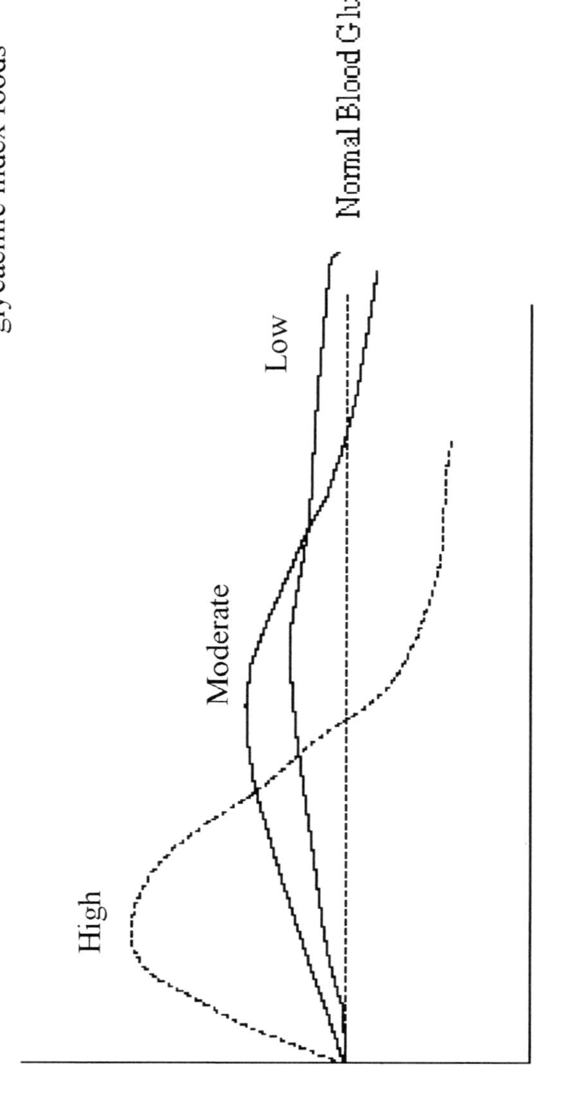

Figure 3. Glycaemic response of high, moderate and low glycaemic index foods

fective in predicting the glucose responses of meals. The variability in glycaemic responses of meals can be influenced by a variety of factors which can confound many studies if they are not carefully controlled.

Food Preparation

The method and degree of processing involved in the preparation of foods is a primary factor in determining the blood glucose response to the food (Walton and Rhodes, 1997). Cooking, grinding, and processing of a carbohydrate food can influence the glycaemic response of the food. (Vaaler, Hanssen, and Aagenaes, 1984; O' Dea, Nestel, and Antonoff, 1980;)

Cooking of carbohydrate foods, particularly starchy foods, can increase the glycaemic index for these foods (Walton and Rhodes, 1997). It has been found that there is a rapid increase in the blood glucose response of potatoes when they are cooked. It appears that with boiling the granules of starch rupture when they swell, making starch more vulnerable to digestive enzymes (Vaaler et al.1984) . The method of preparation affects the glucose response (Walton and Rhodes, 1997). Gatti et al. (1987) found that boiled rice had a greater glucose response than rice that was boiled and then baked. The lower water content of the baked rice probably decreased the glycaemic response.

Grinding and crushing of foods can increase the glycaemic index (Collier and O'Dea, 1982; O'Dea, Nestle, and Antonoff, 1980). Holt and Brand Miller (1994) found that smaller particles of wheat ellict a greater glucose and insulin response. Ground foods have a greater surface area, making the starch more easily digested (O'Dea, Nestle, and Antonoff, 1980; Brand et al. 1985).

The glycaemic response of a food can be altered by the form in which it is consumed. Haber et al.(1977) found that apple juice, pureed apples and whole apples produce the same peak glucose levels. Conversely, blood glucose levels remained elevated longer with the apple than with the pureed apple and for even less time with apple juice.

It has been demonstrated that processed foods produce a greater glycaemic response than foods which are cooked by more traditional means. Processing methods like extrusion cooking, explosion puffing and instantisation make starchy foods more readily digestible (Brand et al.1992).

Fibre

The fibre content of foods can influence the glycaemic index of that food. Fibre decreases the glucose response (Wolever, 1990; Hagander et al., 1984). Soluble fibre has been found to decrease the blood glucose response more than insoluble fibre (Nishimune et al., 1991). Fibre alters the transit time of food through the small intestine. The increased transit time probably decreases the amount of carbohydrate that is absorbed, decreasing the blood glucose response (Walton and Rhodes, 1997).

Fat and Protein

The blood glucose response of carbohydrate is reduced when fat or protein are present (Jenkins et al, 1981; Crapo et al, 1976; Collier and O'Dea,1983; Spiller et al., 1987). Along with decreasing the blood glucose response, protein increases the insulin response (Spiller et al., 1987; Brody, 1994). Increased insulin levels are probably responsible for the lower glucose levels observed when protein is included in a meal. Fat slows gastric emptying. If the food leaves the stomach more slowly the rate at which carbohydrate is available for digestion and absorption is also decreased. While protein can decrease the glycaemic index it seems that very large quantities (approx. 50 g) are needed for this to occur (Nuttall et al., 1984).

Glycaemic Index and Performance in Exercise

Even though the glycaemic index of foods can be affected by several factors, it is still a useful reference guide. The glycaemic index can provide information that may enhance performance and prevent nutritional practices that will hinder performance.

Carbohydrate Intake Before Exercise

Many athletes consume a pre-competition or pre-practice meal. If the meal is eaten two to three hours before the exercise session performance seems to be enhanced. Controversy surrounds the ingestion of carbohydrates 30 to 60 minutes prior to endurance exercise. Several studies (Costill et al., 1977; Hargreaves et al, 1985.) suggest that the intake of carbohydrates at this time increases muscle glycogen utilization during exercise and decrease the time to fatigue in exhaustive exercise (Defrenzo, 1981). The decrease in performance is believed to be the result of elevated blood glucose and insulin levels immediately prior to exercise (Costill et al, 1977). The combination of high concentrations of blood glucose and insulin at the onset of exercise can lead to a dramatic fall in blood glucose to levels below that had no carbohydrates had been ingested (Costill et al., 1977; Hargreaves et al., 1985.). The fall in blood glucose is due to the uptake of glucose by the muscles when insulin levels are increased.

Consuming a low glycaemic index food 30 to 60 minutes prior to exercise may help prevent decreased performance. Thomas et al. (1991). showed an increased time to exhaustion in a continuous steady state exercise session when lentils (low glycaemic index, 29 ± 3) rather than potatoes (high glycaemic, 98 ± 13) or glucose were consumed 1 hour before exercise. The lentils resulted in lower blood glucose levels, compared to potato or glucose, both 30 and 60 minutes after ingestion. Blood glucose was maintained for the lentils at a level above that for glucose and water at the end of exercise. The improvements in performance may have been due to a sparing of muscle glycogen. The high glycaemic index food (potatoes) resulted in higher lactate levels during exercise, and increased carbohydrate oxidation during the first 90 minutes of exercise.

In another study Thomas et al.(1994) had six trained cyclists consume four different meals prior to exercise bouts. Two of the meals, flaked potato and rice cereal, had a high GI, and two had a low GI (flaked lentils, bran cereal). Using the potato feeding as a reference, GI varied as follows: 100 (potato flakes), 73 (rice cereal), 36 (lentil flakes), 30 (bran cereal). Each meal was consumed 60 min before an exercise bout to exhaustion at 65 to 70% VO2max. Blood glucose changes during the 60 min after food ingestion were consistent with the GI values of the foods. Insulin pattern reflected the glycaemic response during the period before exercise but fell to similar levels for all groups during exercise. Free fatty acid use was greatest during the bran cereal trial and the most was used carbohydrate during the potato trial. They concluded that low glycaemic foods produce higher concentrations of blood glucose at the end of exercise and increased free fatty acid levels throughout exercise when compared to high glycaemic index foods. They have suggested that if CHO is consumed within an hour of exercise that low glycaemic index foods would be a better option.

Since many rowers train early in the morning and often eat within an hour of practice, the choice of low glycaemic index foods will help them get through the workout with less fatigue and leave them with more energy for subsequent workouts.

Carbohydrate Intake During Exercise

Carbohydrate consumption during endurance exercise has been

shown to improve performance and increase the time to exhaustion (Murdoch et al. 1993; Coyle et al., 1983; Coyle et al., 1986; Coggan and Coyle, 1987). Unlike the intake of carbohydrate 30 to 60 minutes prior to exercise, the intake of carbohydrate during exercise is not affected by the increase in blood and subsequent release of insulin because insulin release is suppressed by other hormones that are released early in exercise.

The intake of CHO during exercise helps maintain blood sugar levels allowing more of the CHO stored in the muscles and liver to be used by the working muscles. This helps prevent the total CHO depletion that can lead to protein oxidation and overtraining. Since insulin levels are suppressed there does not seem to be any difference between the use of high or low glycaemic index foods during continuous exercise like rowing.

Post-Exercise Carbohydrate Intake

The primary goal of carbohydrate intake after exercise is to replete the body's liver and muscle glycogen stores. This is of particular importance if multiple training sessions are done in a day or during competitions where the athlete may have to race several heats in one day.

Research indicates that high glycaemic index carbohydrates increases the rate of muscle glycogen resynthesis after exercise more than low glycaemic index foods. Kiens et al. (1990) tested the effect of diets of 70% carbohydrate with either low or high glycaemic index for 44 hours following glycogen-depleting exercise. The insulin response to the high glycaemic index diet was 98% higher, even though the blood glucose levels were similar for the two diets. The rate of muscle glycogen resynthesis was twice as fast during the first six hours post exercise with the high glycaemic index diet, but there was no difference in glycogen replacement by 22 hours post exercise.

Burke et al. (1993) fed five elite cyclists diets containing primarily low or high glycaemic index foods for 24 hours after a glycogen-depleting ride. Both diets were similar in total carbohydrate (10 g/kg) which was divided equally among four meals. Blood glucose and insulin were assessed for 90 minutes following each meal. Muscle glycogen increased almost twice as much after 24 hours on the high glycaemic index diet, compared to the low glycaemic index diet.

Conclusion

While carbohydrate stores are not the limiting factor during a single race they can be limiting factors during repeated heats and training. CHO ingestion close to competition or training time should consist of low glycaemic index foods. During training it doesn't matter what type of CHO is consumed but it is important to be taking in some CHO. Following exercise high glycaemic index foods seem to speed recovery and enhance muscle and liver glycogen resynthesis.

Glycaemic Index of Common Foods

High glycaemic index foods are those with a rating of 70 or greater, moderate has a rating of 50 to 70 and low is under 50. Foods listed from highest to lowest glycemic index within category. Glycemic index was calculated using glucose as the reference with GI of 100. Modified from Foster-Powell and Brand Miller (1995).

Breads and Grains

waffle	76	rice, brown	55
doughnut	76	bulgur	48
bagel	72	spaghetti, white	41
wheat bread, white	70	whole wheat	37
bread, whole wheat	69	wheat kernels	41
cornmeal	68	barley	25
bran muffin	60		
rice, white	56		
rice, instant	91		

Cereals

Rice Krispies	82
Grape Nuts Flakes	80
Corn Flakes	77
Cheerios	74
shredded wheat	69
Grape Nuts	67
Life	66
oatmeal	61
All Bran	42

Fruits

watermelon	72
pineapple	66
raisins	64
banana	53
grapes	52
orange	43
pear	36
apple	36

Starchy Vegetables

potatoes, baked	83
potatoes, instant	83
potatoes, mashed	73
carrots	71
sweet potatoes	54
green peas	48

Snacks

rice cakes	82
jelly beans	80
graham crackers	74
corn chips	73
life savers	70
angel food cake	67
wheat crackers	67
popcorn	55
oatmeal cookies	55
potato chips	54
chocolate	49
banana cake	47
peanuts	14

Legumes

baked beans	48
chick peas	33
butter beans	31
lentils	29
kidney beans	27
soy beans	18

Beverages

soft drinks	68
orange juice	57
apple juice	41

Dairy

ice cream	61
yogurt,	33
milk, full fat	27
milk, skim	32

Sugars

honey	73
sucrose	65
lactose	46
fructose	23

References

Blomstrand E, Celsing F, and Newsholme EA (1988). Changes in plasma concentrations of aromatic and branch-chain amino acids during sustained exercise in man and their possible role in fatigue. Acta Physiologica Scandinavica 133, 115-21

Bloomstrand E, Hassmen P, Ekblom B et al (1991). Administration of branch-chain amino acids during sustained exercise - effects on performance and on plasma concentration of some amino acids. European Journal of Applied Physiology 63, 83-8

Bloomstrand E, Hassmen P, and Newsholme E (1991). Effect of branch-chain amino acid supplementation on mental performance. Acta Physiologica Scandinavica 143, 225-6.

Brand JC et al. (1985). Food processing and the glycaeimc index. Am J Clin Nut. 42: 1192-1196.

Brody T. (1994). Nutritional Biochemistry. Academic Press. NY: NY.

Burke LM, Collier GR, and Hargreaves M. (1993). Muscle glycogen storage after prolonged exercise: effect of the glycaemic index of carbohydrate feedings. J Appl Physiol. 75: 1019-1023.

Carli G, Bonifazi M, Lodi L et al (1992). Changes in exercise-induced hormone response to branched chain amino acid administration. European Journal of Applied Physiology 64, 272-7.

Coombes J, and McNaughton L (1995). The effects of branched chain amino acid supplementation on indicators of muscle damage after prolonged strenuous exercise. Medicine and Science in Sports and Exercise 27, S149 (abstract)

Coggan AR, and Coyle EF. Reversal of fatigue during prolonged exercise by carbohydrate infusion or ingestion. J Appl Physiol 1987; 63: 2388-95

Coggan AR. and Coyle EF. Effect of carbohydrate feedings during high intensity intermittent exercise. J Appl Physiol 65: 1703-9

Collier G, and O'Dea K. (1982). Effect of physical form of carbohydrate on postprandial glucose, insulin. and gastric inhibitory peptide response in type 2 diabetes. Am J Clin Nutr. 36: 10-14.

Collier G, and O'Dea K. (1983). The effect of congestion of fat on glucose, insulin, and gastric inhibitory polypeptide responses to carbohydrate and protein. Am J Clin Nutr. 37: 941-944.

Costill DL, Coyle E, Dalsky G, et al. (1977). Effects of elevated plasma FFA and insulin on muscle glvcoi,,en. J Appl Physiol; 43: 695-9.

Coyle EF, Haberiz JM, Hurley BE et al.(1983). Carbohydrate feeding during prolonged strenuous exercise can delay fatitue. J Appl. Physiol. 1983: 55: 230-5

Coyle EF. Coggan AR, et al. (1986) Muscle glycogen utilization during,, prolonged exercise when fed carbohydrate. J Appl Physiol. 61: 165-72

Crapo PA, Reaven G, Olefsky J, et al. (1976). Plasma glucose and insulin responses to orally administered simple and complex carbohydrates. Diabetes. 25: 741-747.

Davis JM (1995). Carbohydrates, branched-chain amino acids, and endurance, The central fatigue hypothesis. International Journal of Sport Nutrition 5, S29-38

Davis JM, Baily SP, Woods JA et al (1992). Effects of carbohydrate feedings on plasma free tryptophan and branched-chain amino acids during prolonged cycling European Journal of Applied Physiology 65, 513-19

Defrenzo RA, Ferrannini E, Sato Y, et al.(1981). Synergistic interaction between exercise and insulin on peripheral glucose intake. J Clin Invest 1981; 68: 1468-74

Febbraio M, and Stewart K. (1996). CHO feeding before prolonged exercise: effect of glycaemic index on muscle glycogenolysis and exercise performance.

Gastmann UA, and Lehmann MJ (1998). Overtraining and the BCAA hypothesis. Medicine and Science in Sports and Exercise 30, 1173-8

Gatti E, Testolin G, Noe D, et al. (1987). Plasma glucose and insulinresponses to carbohydrate food (rice) in different thermal processing. Ann Nutr Metab. 31: 296-303.

Hagander B, Schersten B, Asp N. et al. (1994). Effect of diterary fibre on blood glucose, plasma immunoreactive insulin, C-peptide and GIP responses in non insulin dependent (type 2) diabetics and controls. Acta Med Scand. 15: 205-213.

Hargreaves M, Costill DL, Katz A, et al. (1985). Effect of fructose ingestion on muscle glycogen usage during exercise. Med Sci Sports Exerc: 17: 360-3

Hefler SK, Wildman L, Gaesser GA et al (1993). Branched-chain amino acid (BCAA) supplementation improves endurance performance in competitive cyclists. Medicine and Science in Sports and Exercise 25, S24 (abstract)

Hollenbeck CB, and Coulston AM. (1991) The clinical utility of the glycaemic index and its application to mixed meals. Can J Physiol Pharmacol. 69: 100-107.

Holt SHA, and Brand Miller J. (1995). Increased insulin response to ingested foods associated with lessened satiety. Appetite. 24: 43-54.

Holt SHA, and Brand Miller J.(1994). Particle size, satiety, and the glycaemic response. Eur J Clin Nutr. 48: 496-502.

Jenkins DJA, Wolever TMS, Jenkins AL. et al. (1984) The glycaemic response to carbohydrate foods. Lancet 11: 388-391.

Jenkins DJA, Jenkins AL, Wolever TMS. et al. (1986) Simple and complex carbohydrates. Nutr Rev. 44: 44-49.

Jenkins DJA, Jenkins AL, Wolever TMS. et al. (1994) Low glycaemic index: lente carbohydrates and physiological effects of altered food frequency. Ain J Clin Nutr. 59 Supp].: 706S-709S I.

Kargotich S, Rowbottom DG, Keast D et al (1996). Plasma glutamine changes after high intensity exercise in elite male swimmers. Medicine and Science in Sport and Exercise 28, S133 (abstract)

Kiens, B. A.B. Raven, A.K. Valeur and E.A. Richter (1990). Benefit of dietary simple carbohydrates on the early postexercise muscle glycogen repletion in male athletes (abstract). Med. Sci. Sports Exerc. 22:S88.

Kreider RB (1998). Central fatigue hypothesis and overtraining. In Kreider RB, Fry AC, O'Toole M (editors), Overtraining in Sport (pages 309-31). Champaign, Illinois: Human Kinetics

Kreider RB, Jackson CW (1994). Effects of amino acid supplementation on psychological status during and intercollegiate swim season. Medicine and Science in Sports and Exercise 26, S115 (abstract)

Kreider RB, Miller GW, Mitchell M et al (1992). Effects of amino acid supplementation on ultraendurance triathlon performance. In Proceedings of the I World Congress on Sport Nutrition (pages 488-536). Barcelona, Spain: Enero

Low SY, Taylor PM, Rennie MJ (1996). Responses of glutamine transport in cultured rat skeletal muscle to osmotically induced changes in cell volume. Journal of Physiology 492, 877-85

Murdoch SD, Bazzare TL, Snider IP, et al.(1993) Differences in the effect of carbohydrate food form on endurance performance to exhaustion. Int J Sport Nutr; 3: 41-54

Newsholme EA, Parry-Billings M, McAndrew M et al (1991). Biochemical mechanism to explain some characteristics of over-training. In Brouns F (editor): Medical Sports Science, Vol. 32, Advances in Nutrition and Top Sport (pages 79-93). Basel, Germany: Karger

Newsholme EA,and Calder PC (1997). The proposed role of glutamine in some cells of the immune system and speculative consequences for the whole animal. Nutrition 13, 728-30

Nieman DC, Pedersen BK (1999). Exercise and immune function. Recent developments. Sports Medicine 27, 72-80

Nishimune T, Yakushiji T, Sumimoto T, et al. (1991) Glycaemic response and fibre content of some foods. Am J Clin Nutr. 54: 414-419.

O'Dea K. Nestel PJ, and Antonoff L. (1980). Physical factors influ-

encing postprandial glucose and insulin responses to starch. Am J Clin Nutr. 33: 760-765.

Parry-Billings M, Blomstrand E, Leighton B et al (1990). Does endurance exercise impair glutamine metabolism? Canadian Journal of Sport Science 13, 13P (abstract)

Parry-Billings M, Blomstrand E, McAndrew N et al (1990). A communicational link between skeletal muscle, brain and cells of the immune system. International Journal of Sports Medicine 11, S122-8

Parry-Billings M, Budgett R, Koutedakis K et al (1992). Plasma amino acid concentrations in the overtraining syndrome: Possible effects on the immune system. Medicine and Science in Sports and Exercise 24, 1353-8

Rennie MJ (1996). Glutamine metabolism and transport in skeletal muscle and heart and their clinical relevance. Journal of Nutrition 126(4), 1142S-9S

Rennie MJ, Tadros L, Khogali S et al (1994). Glutamine transport and its metabolic effects. Journal of Nutrition 124, 1503S-8S

Rohde T, Asp S, MacLean DA et al (1998). Competitive sustained exercise in humans, lymphokine activated killer cell activity, and glutamine--an intervention study. European Journal of Applied Physiology 78, 448-53

Spiller GA, Jensen CD, Pattison TS, et al. (1987). Effect of protein on serum glucose and insulin response to sugars. Am J Clin Nutr. 46: 474-480.

Thomas, D.E., J.R. Brotherhood and J.C. Brand (1991). Carbohydrate feeding before exercise: effect of glycemic index. Int. J. Sports Med. 112:180-186.

Thomas, D.E., J.R. Brotherhood and J.Brand Miller (1994). Plasma glucose levels after prolonged strenuous exercise correlate inversely with glycemic response to food consumed before exercise. Int. J. Sport Nutr. 4:361-373.

Varnier M, Leese GP, Thompson J et al (1995). Stimulatory effect of glutamine on glycogen accumulation in human skeletal muscle. American Journal of Physiology 269, E309-15

Wagenmakers AJ (1998). Muscle amino acid metabolism at rest and during exercise: role in human physiology and metabolism. In Holloszy JO (editor): Exercise and Sport Sciences Reviews (pages 287-314). Baltimore, Maryland: Williams & Wilkins

Walton P, Rhodes, EC. (1997). Glycaemic index and optimal performance. Sports Med. 23(3): 164-172.

Wolever TMS. Jenkins DJA, Jenkins AL, et al. (1991) The glycaemic index: methodology and clinical implications. Ain J Clin Nutr. 54: 846-854.

Wolever TMS. (1992). Glycaemic index versus glycaemic response.Diabetes Care.15: 1436-1437.

Wolever TMS. Relationship between dietary fibre and composition in foods and the glycaemic index. Am J Clin Nutr. 51: 72-75.

A

aerobic system 25, 225, 227
Aerobic threshold 27, 29
anaerobic alactic system 154, 189, 225
anaerobic glycolysis 191, 225, 227
anaerobic threshold 27, 29

B

Blood Lactate analysis 59
    Pre- Test procedure 62
    Test Performance 63
    Wattages 64

C

Caffeine 196
    Adverse Effects 198
    Caffeine content 197
    Legal Issues 198
    Recommendations 199
carbohydrate 196, 215, 217, 218, 227, 237
    after exercise 245
    Before Exercise 243
    carbohydrate 244
Circuit training 155
Conconi Method 70
Creatine 188
    Adverse effects 192
    Creatine supplementation 190
    Legal Issues 193

Practical implications for Rowers 192
Recommendations 193

D

dehydration 214, 216
drug testing 185, 188, 198, 213

E

Energy Requirements 231
    Daily Energy Requirements 233
    Energy cost of training 232
Energy Systems 225
    and Muscle Fibre Types 227
    Integration of Energy Systems 227

F

fat 196, 217, 218, 227, 236, 242
Fat Burners 203
Field/Performance Testing 80
Flexibility 158
    and age 161
    and gender 160

G

Gas Exchange Methods 68
Ginseng 203
Glutamine 193, 234

Adverse Effects 195

Legal Issues 195

Recommendations 196

Glycaemic Index 238

and Performance 243

Fibre 242

Food Preparation 241

Glycaemic Index of Common Foods 247

Post-Exercise 245

Goal Setting 88

and Macrocycles 94

Establishing Goals 88

Following up 89

Golgi Tendon Organs 149

H

Heart Rate 72

Determination of Heart Rate 73

Maximum Heart Rate 75

I

Iron 200

Adverse Effects 202

Iron requirements 201

Legal Issues 202

Recommendations 202

K

Kcal 218, 231

L

Lactate 154
    Exercise and 27

M

Macrocycles 93
    Goal Setting 94
    Length 93
Microcycle 99
    Alternate load 100
    End loaded 99
    Even load 101
    Front loaded 99
    Pyramidal loading 102
Muscle Fibre Type 109, 227
    Fast twitch glycolytic 109, 229
    Fast twitch oxidative-glycolytic 109, 229
    Slow twitch 109, 229
    undifferentiated fast twitch 110, 229
muscle spindles 149

P

Prebuescent Strength Training
    Benefits and risks
    Program design
    Rate of Progression 145
    Recommendations
    Strength increases
    Training adaptations

protein 217, 218, 227, 234, 236, 242

S

Skill Learning
  Classification of Skills 141
  Organizing a Practice 144
    Duration of Practice 146
    Feedback 145
    Frequency of Practice 146
    Pre-Practice Preparation 144
    Types of Practice 147
      Random vs. Blocked Practice 148
      Whole vs. Part Practice 147
  Stages of Skill Learning 142
    Autonomous Stage 143
    Motor Stage 143
    Verbal-Cognitive Stage 142
  Timing and Accuracy 149
Sodium Bicarbonate 186
  Adverse Effects 187
  Legal Issues 188
  Recommendations 188
  Sodium Bicarbonate Supplementation 186
Steroid Replacements 203
Strength Training 107
  and Prepubescent rowers 125
  and Skill Development 139
    Circuit versus Traditional 155
    Intensity 154
    Rest and Recovery 154
    Selection of Exercises 154
    Sets and Reps 152
  Competitive Phase 120

General Preparation Phase 111, 112
Intensity 111, 112, 117, 119, 120
Pre-Competitive Phase 119
Sets 112, 117, 120, 121
Specific Preparation Phase 116
Strength Levels 108
Volume 112, 117, 120
Stretching 163
Dynamic 163
PNF 166
Static 165

T

Tapering
Duration 177
Intensity 177
Training Frequency 176
Training Volume 174
Training Categories 25
Category II 44
Category III 42
Category IV 37
Category V 35
Category VI 32
Training Plan 87
Competitive phase 91, 120
Pre-Competitive Phase 91, 117
Preparatory Phase 90, 111, 116
Transition Phase 92

V

vestibular system 150
visual system 150
Vitamins and Minerals 199
    Adverse Effects 200
    Legal Issues 200
    Recommendations 200
VO2 max 14, 25, 30, 43, 44, 68, 214

W

Warm up 13, 63, 70
    Designing a warm up 16
    Injury prevention 15
    Pre race Warm up 18
    Types of warm ups 15
Weight Loss 203
    Gradual Weight Loss 217
    Rapid Weight Loss 213
      Effects on Performance 158, 214

About the Author

Ed McNeely, M.Sc. is the President of the Sport Performance Institute Inc., amultinational company dedicated to the development and education of high performance athletes and coaches. Ed has acted as a consultant to 17 Olympic and professional sports teams.

He has been a regular presenter at rowing conferences in both Canada and th U.S. Ed is a regular contributor to RCA magazine and Independant Rowing News. He has written the strength training components of the Rowing Canada Aviron coaching certification program.